WALKING
MILAN

WALKING

MILAN

THE BEST OF THE CITY

Fabrizia Villa

NATIONAL GEOGRAPHIC

Washington, D.C.

WALKING MILAN

CONTENTS

PART 1

PAGE 12
WHIRLWIND TOURS

PART 2

PAGE 36
MILAN'S NEIGHBORHOODS

PART 3

PAGE 176
TRAVEL ESSENTIALS

Previous pages:
Galleria Vittorio
Emanuele II
Left: Piazza del
Duomo
Top right:
portrait of San
Carlo Borromeo
Center: Castello
Sforzesco
Right: A design
for the facade
of the Duomo

Introduction

Italy spoils us in many ways, not least in its towns and cities, which are a joy to explore on foot. Watery Venice, ancient Rome, Renaissance Florence all have glorious historic hearts and labyrinths of stage-set perfection. But Milan? Milan is a little different, at least at first glance: a business and fashion center that can seem a more modern, workaday city than its illustrious neighbors—up to a point. One of the beauties of walking is slowing down and looking harder at your surroundings. Do this in Milan and the rewards come quickly. Few other cities have as thrilling a centerpiece as Milan's great Gothic cathedral, the Duomo; or, just a few steps away, as pretty a shopping arcade as the 19th-century Galleria Vittorio Emanuele II; or, only a few steps farther, as celebrated an opera house as La Scala. And it takes only a slightly longer walk before you encounter any number of art-filled churches, superlative museums, and wonderful fashion stores. Our guide, of course, will take you to these attractions, but also to castles, canals, parks, fantastic restaurants, and masterpieces of architecture; everything that makes Milan a great city to explore on foot.

"Ritratto di dama" ("Portrait of Young Woman") by Pollaiolo circa 1470, now the symbol of the Poldi Pezzoli Museum

Tim Jepson,
National Geographic contributor

Visiting Milan

Milan is known as a capital of fashion, finance, and design, but it also has a cultural and historical heritage as rich as any in Europe, with a wealth of churches, palaces, and galleries. At its center rises Italy's finest Gothic cathedral, and among its treasures is one of the world's great paintings, Leonardo da Vinci's "The Last Supper."

VISITING MILAN

Milan in a Nutshell

Milan owes much of its prosperity past and present to its position on fertile plains at the crossroads of northern Italy and close to passes through the Alps to the rest of Western Europe. Founded by the Celts, it became a leading Roman and later Renaissance city, dominated through much of the Middle Ages by great families such as the Sforza and Visconti. After long periods of Spanish and Austrian occupation, Milan became a major industrial center and, latterly, Italy's leading financial and business hub.

Navigating Milan

Milan looks and feels like a more modern city than Rome, Florence, or Venice, but its historic core retains fine monuments to its medieval past. Getting around this area, which centers on the Duomo (cathedral), is easy on foot. Many, but not all, of the key sights, notably the Scala opera house, Santo Stefano church, and Ambrosiana art gallery, are in this district; others, like Castello Sforzesco and Brera art gallery, require longer walks; some— notably Leonardo's "The Last Supper"—may be better reached on public transit.

Milan Day-by-Day

Open every day Museo Teatrale alla Scala.

Monday Many museums are closed, except for Museo Poldi Pezzoli and Museo Teatrale alla Scala. Exhibitions at Palazzo Reale and Museo del Novecento are open only in the afternoon, while MUBA opens in the morning and closes at 3:30 p.m.

Tuesday Most museums are open. Poldi Pezzoli, Villa Necchi Campiglio, and Hangar Bicocca are closed.

Wednesday Hangar Bicocca is closed.

Thursday All museums are open. Palazzo Reale, Museo del Novecento, and Gallerie d'Italia close at 10:30 p.m.

Friday Free entrance to the museums of the Castello Sforzesco from 2 p.m. to 5:30 p.m.

Saturday Palazzo Reale and Museo del Novecento close at 10:30 p.m. Casa del Manzoni is closed.

Sunday Casa del Manzoni is closed.

Clothing trends are set during Milan's twice-yearly Fashion Week, with shows at venues throughout the city and models walking the streets.

Milan on Transit

Milan's transit—especially its trams—can be a fun way to see the city and helpful if you want to avoid walking to more distant sights. The system is integrated: One ticket is valid for 90 minutes across buses and trams, or one journey on the four-line (1, 2, 3, and 5, each color-coded) Metropolitana or Metro (subway) network. Buy tickets from tobacconists (*tabacchi*—look for the white-blue "T" sign), kiosks at transit hubs, or from Metro stations. Visit the transit website *atm.it* or download the free ATM Milano app for more information.

Other Practicalities

The website *turismo.milano.it* is a great source for visitor information, including the latest events and exhibitions; you can even download official tourism apps. If you'll be using taxis, note that licensed taxis are white with an identifying number. They are hard to hail on the street: use stands or call instead *(tel 02 8585 or 02 4040)*. Another option is to use the city's extensive shared bike scheme; visit *bikemi.com* for more information. Finally, be aware that to see "The Last Supper" you need to book months in advance (see pp. 134–135).

Using This Guide

Each tour is plotted on a map and has been planned to fill a day, taking into account opening hours and the times of day when sites are less crowded. Many finish up close to restaurants or lively night spots for evening activities.

USING THIS GUIDE

Whirlwind Tours

Whirlwind Tours are for people who have only a day or a weekend to spend in the city and want to be sure that they see the best of the best. Choose your tour based on your time and interests: One Day, Weekend (Day 1 & Day 2), Milan for Fun, Milan With Kids, or Shopping in Milan.

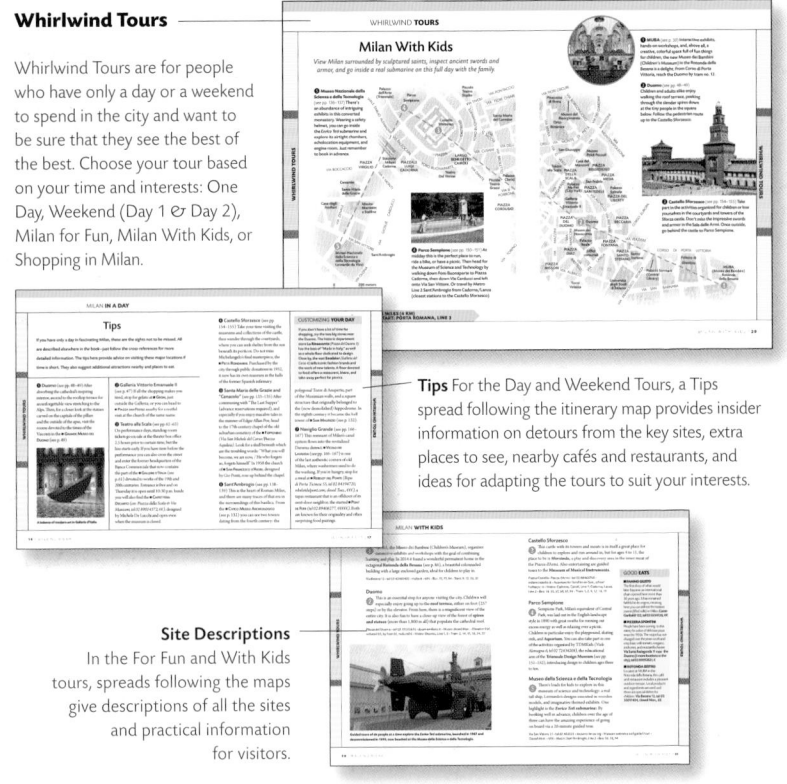

Tips For the Day and Weekend Tours, a Tips spread following the itinerary map provides insider information on detours from the key sites, extra places to see, nearby cafés and restaurants, and ideas for adapting the tours to suit your interests.

Site Descriptions In the For Fun and With Kids tours, spreads following the maps give descriptions of all the sites and practical information for visitors.

Neighborhood Tours

The nine neighborhood tours each begin with an introduction, followed by an itinerary map highlighting the key sites that make up the tour and detailed descriptions of them. Each tour is followed by an "in-depth" spread showcasing one major site along the route, a "distinctly" Milan spread providing background information on a quintessential element of that neighborhood, and a "best of" spread that groups sites thematically.

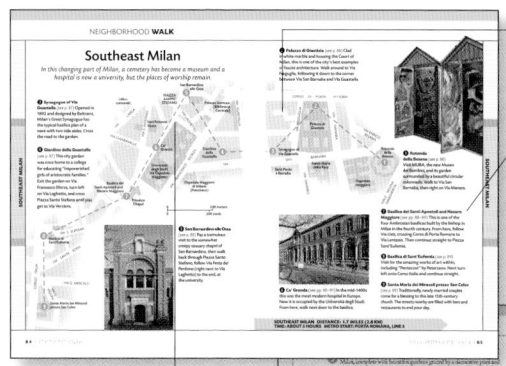

Itinerary Map A map of the neighborhood shows the locations of the key sites.

Captions These briefly describe the key sites and give instructions on finding the next site on the tour. Page references direct you to full descriptions of the key sites on the following pages.

Route Dotted lines link the key sites.

Key Sites Descriptions These provide a detailed description and highlights for each site, following the order on the map, plus the site's address, website, telephone number, entrance fee, days closed, and nearest Metro station and bus stops.

Good Eats Refer to these lists for a selection of cafés and restaurants along the tour.

Price Ranges for Key Sites

€	€1–€5
€€	€5–€8
€€€	€8–€13
€€€€	€13–€18
€€€€€	over €18

Prices Ranges for Good Eats (for one person, excluding drinks)

€	Under €15
€€	€15–€25
€€€	€25–€40
€€€€	€40–€60
€€€€€	over €60

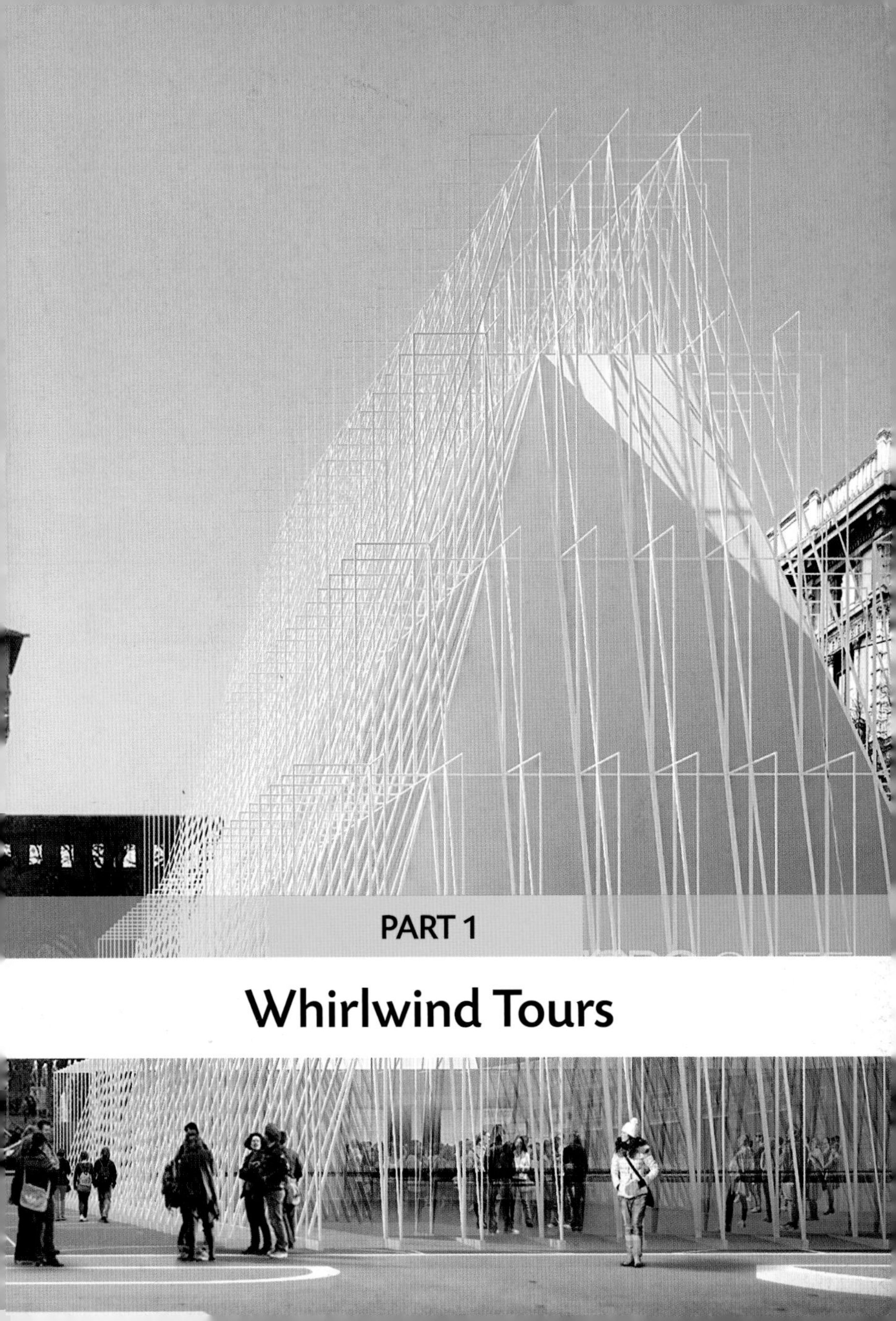

PART 1

Whirlwind Tours

Milan in a Day

Experience Milan's most important churches, the museums of the Castello Sforzesco, and the city's old-world waterways.

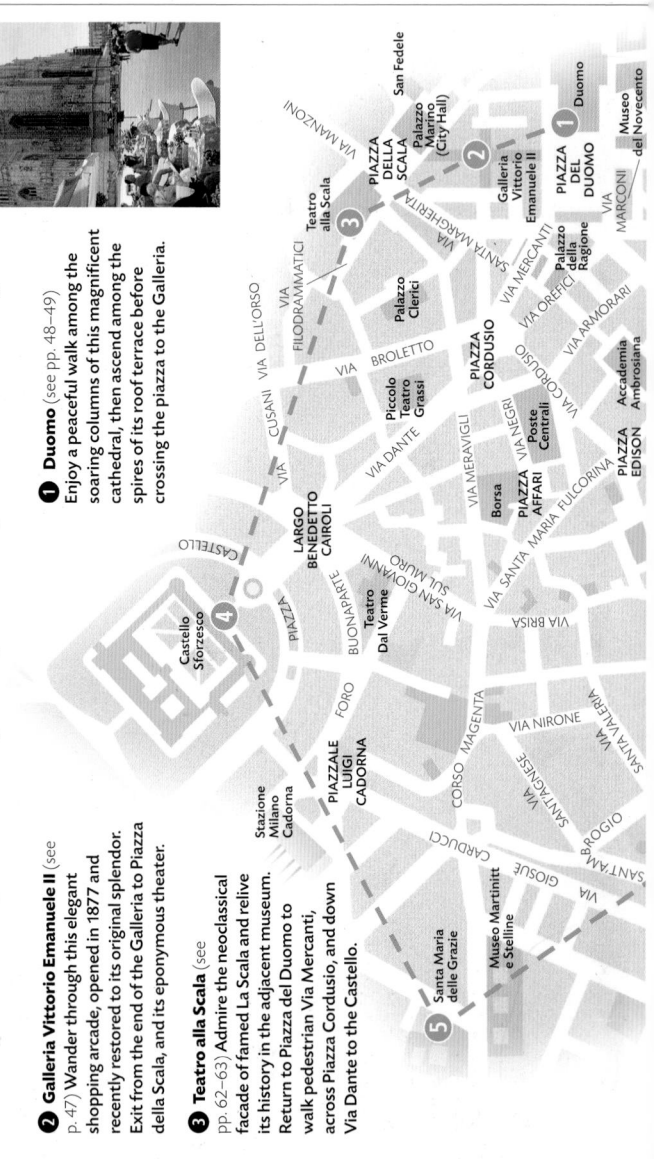

❶ Duomo (see pp. 48–49)
Enjoy a peaceful walk among the soaring columns of this magnificent cathedral, then ascend among the spires of its roof terrace before crossing the piazza to the Galleria.

❷ Galleria Vittorio Emanuele II (see p. 47) Wander through this elegant shopping arcade, opened in 1877 and recently restored to its original splendor. Exit from the end of the Galleria to Piazza della Scala, and its eponymous theater.

❸ Teatro alla Scala (see pp. 62–63) Admire the neoclassical facade of famed La Scala and relive its history in the adjacent museum. Return to Piazza del Duomo to walk pedestrian Via Mercanti, across Piazza Cordusio, and down Via Dante to the Castello.

Map labels:
VIA MANZONI · San Fedele · PIAZZA DELLA SCALA · Palazzo Marino (City Hall) · Teatro alla Scala · VIA SANTA MARGHERITA · Galleria Vittorio Emanuele II · PIAZZA DEL DUOMO · ❶ Duomo · VIA MARCONI · Museo del Novecento · Palazzo della Ragione · VIA ORILIFICI · VIA ARMORARI · Accademia Ambrosiana · VIA FILODRAMMATICI · VIA CUSANI · VIA DELL'ORSO · Palazzo Clerici · VIA BROLETTO · Piccolo Teatro Grassi · PIAZZA CORDUSIO · VIA DANTE · VIA MERAVIGLI · VIA NEGRI · Poste Centrali · Borsa · PIAZZA AFFARI · PIAZZA EDISON · VIA SANTA MARIA FULCORINA · VIA SAN GIOVANNI SUL MURO · LARGO BENEDETTO CAIROLI · Teatro Dal Verme · PIAZZA CASTELLO · Castello Sforzesco ❹ · FORO BUONAPARTE · PIAZZALE LUIGI CADORNA · Stazione Milano Cadorna · CORSO MAGENTA · VIA NIRONE · VIA BRISA · VIA SANT'AGNESE · VIA SANTA VALERIA · VIA CARDUCCI · VIA GIOSUE · VIA SANT'AMBROGIO · Museo Martinitt e Stelline · ❺ Santa Maria delle Grazie

MILAN IN A DAY   DISTANCE: 2.5 MILES (4 KM)
TIME: ABOUT 8 HOURS   METRO START: DUOMO, LINE 1

4 Castello Sforzesco
(see pp. 154–155) Explore the former home of Milan's 15th-century ruling family, now housing several fascinating museums. After a rest in its beautiful courtyards, walk down Foro Buonaparte, across Piazzale Cadorna, then down Via Carducci and turn right on Corso Magenta.

5 Santa Maria delle Grazie and "Cenacolo" (see pp. 133–135) Visit the splendid Renaissance church designed by Guiniforte Solari and later expanded by Bramante, and (with advance reservations) see the "Cenacolo" ("The Last Supper") painted by Leonardo in the convent refectory. From here, go along Via Zenale and Via San Vittore to Piazza Sant'Ambrogio.

6 Sant'Ambrogio (see pp. 138–139) Through its superb portico, enter the basilica founded in the fourth century by Sant'Ambrogio, patron saint of the city along with San Carlo Borromeo and San Galdino. Walk down Via de Amicis and then turn right down Corso di Porta Ticinese to Piazza XXIV Maggio. Naviglio Grande is just across the square, on the right.

7 Naviglio Grande (see pp. 166–167) The Navigli are artificial waterways, popular for sunset strolls, lined with bars and restaurants, and a great stop for an *aperitivo* (see pp. 80–81).

VIA SAN VITTORE
PIAZZA SANT'AMBROGIO
PIAZZA
Università Cattolica
Sant'Ambrogio
VIA SAN PIO V
VIA DEL TORCHIO
VIA CAPPUCCIO
VIA SANT'ORSOLA
CORSO GENOVA
VIA LANZONE
VIA TORINO
VIA MAZZINI
PIAZZA RESISTENZA PARTIGIANA
VIA CONCA DEL NAVIGLIO
VIA E. DE AMICIS
RIPA DI PORTA TICINESE
VIALE GORIZIA
VIALE G.
D'ANNUNZIO
VIA OLINZIO
VIA ARENA
CORSO DI PORTA TICINESE
7 Naviglio Grande
PIAZZA XXIV MAGGIO
PIAZZA DIAZ
Palazzo Reale
VIA TORINO

0   200 meters
0   200 yards

Tips

If you have only a day in fascinating Milan, these are the sights not to be missed. All are described elsewhere in the book—just follow the cross-references for more detailed information. The tips here provide advice on visiting these major locations if time is short. They also suggest additional attractions nearby and places to eat.

❶ **Duomo** (see pp. 48–49) After absorbing the cathedral's inspiring interior, ascend to the rooftop terrace for an unforgettable view stretching to the Alps. Then, for a closer look at the statues carved on the capitals of the pillars and the outside of the apse, visit the rooms devoted to the times of the Visconti in the ■ Grande Museo del Duomo (see p. 49)

A balance of modern art in Gallerie d'Italia

❷ **Galleria Vittorio Emanuele II** (see p. 47) If all the shopping makes you tired, stop for gelato at ■ Grom, just outside the Galleria; or you can head to ■ Piazza san Fedele nearby for a restful visit at the church of the same name.

❸ **Teatro alla Scala** (see pp. 62–63) On performance days, standing-room tickets go on sale at the theater box office 2.5 hours prior to curtain time, but the line starts early. If you have time before the performance you can also cross the street and enter the former headquarters of the Banca Commerciale that now contains the part of the ■ Gallerie d'Italia (see p. 61) devoted to works of the 19th and 20th centuries. Entrance is free and on Thursday it is open until 10:30 p.m. Inside you will also find the ■ Caffetteria Decanto (cnr. Piazza della Scala & Via Manzoni, tel 02 89014372, €€), designed by Michele De Lucchi and open even when the museum is closed.

WHIRLWIND TOURS

❹ Castello Sforzesco (see pp. 154–155) Take your time visiting the museums and collections of the castle, then wander through the courtyards, where you can seek shelter from the sun beneath its porticos. Do not miss Michelangelo's final masterpiece, the ■ PIETÀ RONDANINI. Purchased by the city through public donations in 1952, it now has its own museum in the halls of the former Spanish infirmary.

❺ Santa Maria delle Grazie and "Cenacolo" (see pp. 133–135) After communing with "The Last Supper" (advance reservations required), and especially if you enjoy macabre tales in the manner of Edgar Allan Poe, head to the 17th-century chapel of the old suburban cemetery of the ■ FOPPONINO (*Via San Michele del Carso/Piazza Aquileia*). Look for a skull beneath which are the troubling words: "What you will become, we are now, / He who forgets us, forgets himself." In 1958 the church of ■ SAN FRANCESCO D'ASSISI, designed by Gio Ponti, rose up behind the chapel.

❻ Sant'Ambrogio (see pp. 138–139) This is the heart of Roman Milan, and there are many traces of that era in the surroundings of this basilica. From the ■ CIVICO MUSEO ARCHEOLOGICO (see p. 132) you can see two towers dating from the fourth century: the

CUSTOMIZING YOUR DAY

If you don't have a lot of time for shopping, try the two big stores near the Duomo. The historic department store **La Rinascente** (*Piazza del Duomo 3*) has the best of "Made in Italy," as well as a whole floor dedicated to design. Close by, the vast **Excelsior** (*Galleria del Corso 4*) sells iconic fashion brands and the work of new talents. A floor devoted to food offers a restaurant, bistro, and take-away perfect for picnics.

polygonal Torre di Ansperto, part of the Maximian walls, and a square structure that originally belonged to the (now demolished) hippodrome. In the eighth century it became the bell tower of ■ SAN MAURIZIO (see p. 132).

❼ Naviglio Grande (see pp. 166–167) This remnant of Milan's canal system flows into the revitalized Darsena district. ■ VICOLO DEI LAVANDAI (see pp. 166–167) is one of the last authentic corners of old Milan, where washermen used to do the washing. If you're hungry, stop for a meal at ■ REBELOT DEL PONTE (*Ripa di Porta Ticinese 55, tel 02 84194720, rebelotdelpont.com, closed Tues., €€€*), a tapas restaurant that is an offshoot of its next-door neighbor, the starred ■ PONT DE FERR (*tel 02 89406277, €€€€€*). Both are known for their originality and often surprising food pairings.

Milan in a Weekend

The day starts at the Duomo and ends in a lively district near the basilicas of San Lorenzo and Sant'Eustorgio.

7 Basilica di Sant'Ambrogio (see pp. 138–139) **The most** important of the Ambrosian basilicas preserves the remains of the popular saint. Follow Via de Amicis then turn right on Corso di Porta Ticinese. The park is just behind San Lorenzo and Sant'Eustorgio.

6 Santa Maria delle Grazie and "Cenacolo" (see pp. 133–135) **Go inside** and follow the architectural development of the church: from Solari's late Gothic to the grand Renaissance tribune of Bramante. From here, go along Via Zenale and Via San Vittore and continue to Piazza Sant'Ambrogio.

5 San Maurizio al Monastero Maggiore (see p. 132) **Don't be fooled** by the simplicity of the facade. Enter and you will be overwhelmed by the quantity and quality of the frescoes. Next, follow Corso Magenta to Santa Maria delle Grazie.

8 Parco delle Basiliche (see pp. 164, 170–171) **Enjoy a pleasant walk** in the park linking two cornerstones of Milan's spirituality: San Lorenzo, from the early Christian era, and the Romanesque Sant'Eustorgio. End your day at a popular meeting spot, the Colonne di San Lorenzo, on a pedestrian square lively with bars, restaurants, and music.

4 Pinacoteca Ambrosiana (see pp. 122–123) **This** world-class collection has masterpieces by Caravaggio, Leonardo, Botticelli, and more set in a palazzo setting. Continue down Via Spadari and Via Armorari to Via Santa Maria Segreta, and Corso Magenta.

**MILAN IN A WEEKEND DAY 1   DISTANCE: 2.8 MILES (4.5 KM)
TIME: ABOUT 8 HOURS   METRO START: MISSORI, LINE 3**

① Duomo (see pp. 48–49) A visit to the impressive cathedral is a must for its architecture and the wealth and variety of sculptures and stained-glass windows; be sure to take in the delightful roof terrace.

San Maurizio al Monastero Maggiore

VIA MERAVIGLI

VIA S. M. FULCORINA

VIA ANSPERTO

VIA BRISA

VIA NEGRI

⑤

PIAZZA AFFARI

Poste Centrali

VIA CORDUSIO

VIA DEI MERCANTI

Galleria Vittorio Emanuele II

VIA OREFICI

PIAZZA DEL DUOMO

Duomo **①**

VIA ARMORARI

VIA VIGNA

Pinacoteca Ambrosiana

④

③

Santa Maria presso San Satiro

VIA MAZZINI

②

Palazzo dell'Arengario

Palazzo Arcivescovile

Museo del Novecento

Palazzo Reale

VIA MORIGI

SANT'ORSOLA

VIA CAPPUCCIO

VIA CIRCO

VIA SAN MAURILIO

VIA SANTA MARTA

PIAZZA DIAZ

Uffici comunali

VIA SAN PIO V

VIA DEL TORCHIO

VIA TORINO

VIA STAMPA

VIA S VITO

TICINESE

VIA CORRENTI

PORTA TICINESE

PIAZZA DELLA VETRA

Basilica San Lorenzo Maggiore

Santa Maria della Vittoria

DI

CORSO

VIA ARENA

⑧

Parco delle Basiliche

③ Santa Maria presso San Satiro (see p. 117) Here Bramante created one of the most famous optical illusions in art history. Cross the street and head down Via Spadari.

② Museo del Novecento (see p. 46) Italian art of the 20th century centers this impressive new museum in the Palazzo dell'Arengario, on the left side of Piazza del Duomo. Next walk down Via Torino to find Santa Maria presso San Satiro at no. 19.

Milan in a Weekend

Discover the peace of Parco Sempione, go shopping in the Fashion District, and enjoy the beauty of Renaissance Milan.

WHIRLWIND TOURS

0	200 meters
0	200 yards

Palazzo dell'Arte (Triennale)

Parco Sempione

Piccolo Teatro Studio

VIALE EMILIO ALEMAGNA

VIA PALEOCAPA

Castello Sforzesco

CASTELLO

FORO BUONAPARTE

PIAZZA

LARGO BENEDETTO CAIROLI

❶ Castello Sforzesco (see pp. 154–155) **Start** your day at the palace of the Sforzas and its fine museums, then enjoy a walk through the greenery of Parco Sempione, bearing left to reach the Triennale.

❷ Triennale (see pp. 151–152) **Enter the Palazzo dell'Arte and enjoy a special exhibit or the design museum's permanent collection (or both). Then take bus no. 61 four stops to Brera.

❸ Pinacoteca di Brera (see pp. 106–107) **The "Lamentation of Christ" by Mantegna, the "Marriage of the Virgin" by Raphael, and the "Brera Madonna" by Piero della Francesca alone are worth a visit to this treasure chest of masterpieces coveted by Napoleon Bonaparte. Next walk around the building, down Via Fiori Oscuri, right onto Via Borgonuovo, and straight ahead down Via Montenapoleone to the Fashion District.

**MILAN IN A WEEKEND DAY 2 DISTANCE: 2.1 MILES (3.4 KM)
TIME: ABOUT 8 HOURS METRO START: CAIROLI, LINE 1**

❼ Galleria Vittorio Emanuele II (see p. 47) End your day choosing among the high-end shops and restaurants of this elegant vaulted arcade.

❻ Teatro alla Scala (see pp. 62–63) If you have tickets, enjoy the performance. If not, admire the square and floodlit theater. Then turn left into the Galleria.

❺ Museo Poldi Pezzoli (see p. 58) The house-museum of 19th-century aristocrat Gian Giacomo Poldi Pezzoli is a treasury of fine paintings and decorative art. Walk to the end of Via Manzoni to Piazza della Scala.

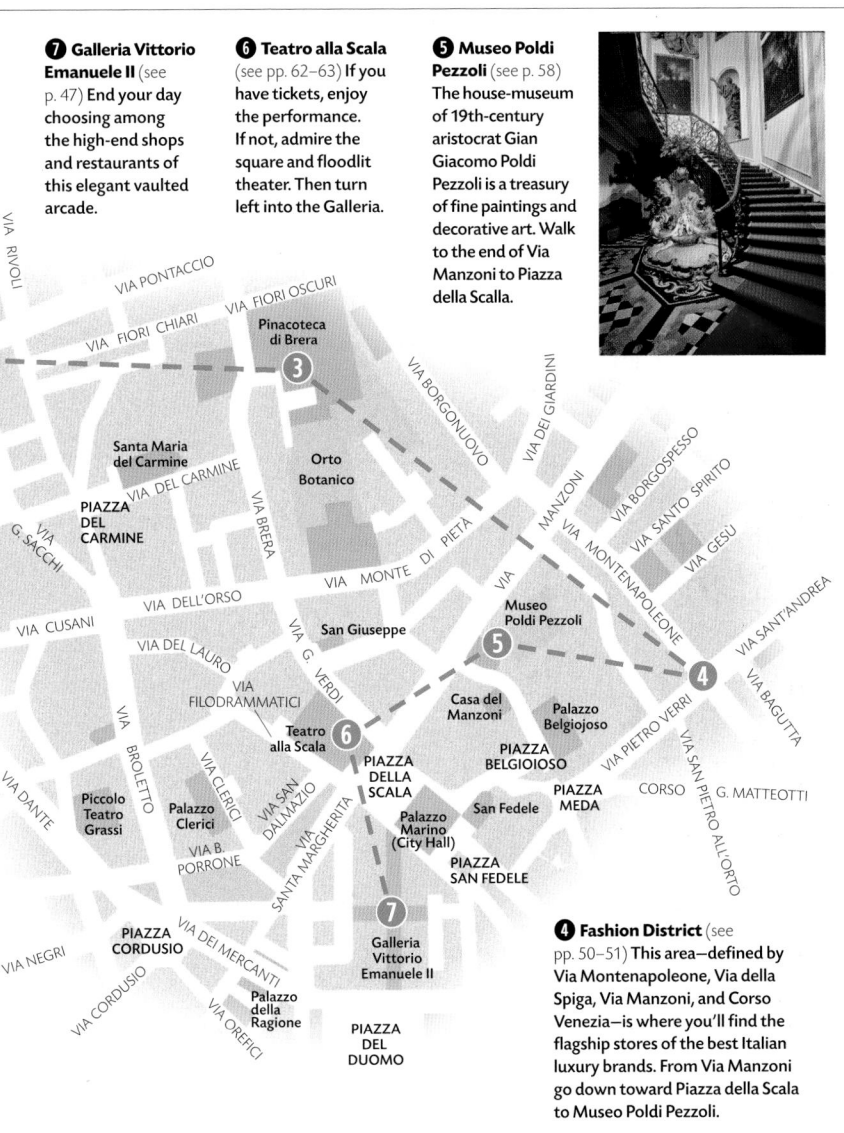

VIA RIVOLI
VIA PONTACCIO
VIA FIORI CHIARI
VIA FIORI OSCURI
Pinacoteca di Brera
③
VIA BORGONUOVO
VIA DEI GIARDINI

Santa Maria del Carmine
Orto Botanico
VIA DEL CARMINE
VIA BRERA
VIA MONTE DI PIETA
VIA MANZONI
VIA BORGOSPESSO
VIA SANTO SPIRITO
VIA MONTENAPOLEONE
VIA GESÙ

PIAZZA DEL CARMINE
VIA G. SACCHI
VIA DELL'ORSO
VIA CUSANI
VIA DEL LAURO

San Giuseppe
VIA G. VERDI

Museo Poldi Pezzoli
⑤
VIA SANT'ANDREA

VIA FILODRAMMATICI
VIA BROLETTO
VIA CLERICI
VIA SAN DALMAZIO
VIA SANTA MARGHERITA

Teatro alla Scala
⑥
PIAZZA DELLA SCALA

Casa del Manzoni
Palazzo Belgioioso
PIAZZA BELGIOIOSO

④
VIA BAGUTTA
VIA PIETRO VERRI
VIA SAN PIETRO ALL'ORTO

VIA DANTE
Piccolo Teatro Grassi
Palazzo Clerici
VIA B. PORRONE

Palazzo Marino (City Hall)
San Fedele
PIAZZA MEDA
CORSO G. MATTEOTTI

PIAZZA SAN FEDELE

VIA NEGRI
PIAZZA CORDUSIO
VIA DEI MERCANTI
Galleria Vittorio Emanuele II
⑦

VIA CORDUSIO
Palazzo della Ragione
VIA OREFICI

PIAZZA DEL DUOMO

④ Fashion District (see pp. 50–51) This area—defined by Via Montenapoleone, Via della Spiga, Via Manzoni, and Corso Venezia—is where you'll find the flagship stores of the best Italian luxury brands. From Via Manzoni go down toward Piazza della Scala to Museo Poldi Pezzoli.

WHIRLWIND TOURS

Tips

Two days in Milan can encompass most of the city's important sights, as well as a few impressive smaller destinations. Follow the page references for detailed information, and use these tips to customize your weekend and visit some lesser known sites along the way.

WHIRLWIND TOURS

DAY 1

❶ Duomo (see pp. 16, 48–49)

❷ Museo del Novecento (see p. 46) After having your fill of the art of the last century, step back in time at the ■ CHURCH OF SAN GOTTARDO IN CORTE (*Via Pecorari*), a Gothic masterpiece built by Azzone Visconti as a chapel for his new palace (now the Palazzo Reale).

❸ Santa Maria presso San Satiro (see p. 117) As lunch approaches, let yourself be tempted by ■ PECK (*Via Spadari 9, tel 02 8023161, €€€€*), a deluxe food and wine store serving well-heeled Milanese for more than a century. Or, for gastronomic delights from the South Tyrol, head to ■ DELICATESSEN (*Piazza Santa Maria Beltrade, tel 02 8051020, closed Sun., €€€*). Once fortified, visit ■ MUSEO FRANCESCO MESSINA (*Via San Sisto 4, tel 02 8645300S, closed Mon.*), a gem opened in 1974 in the famed artist's former studio, the deconsecrated church of San Sisto.

❹ Pinacoteca Ambrosiana (see pp. 122–123) In this recently restored square, home of the stunning art collections of the Ambrosiana, stands the new ■ LEONARDO ICON, a tribute by Daniel Libeskind.

❺ San Maurizio al Monastero Maggiore (see p. 132) On the opposite side of Corso Magenta, ■ PALAZZO LITTA (*Corso Magenta 24, tel 02 8055882, open special weekends only*) offers the most striking example of Lombardy baroque. Rarely open to the public, it holds the Teatro Litta, the oldest theater still active in Milan.

❻ Parco delle Basiliche (see pp. 164, 170–171) After walking the park, lose yourself in the coolest, most fragrant garden in Milan, the historic ■ VIVAIO SORELLE RIVA (*Via Arena in front of no. 7, tel 02 58101141, closed Sun.*). For another place with atmosphere, stop for a meal at the ■ DROGHERIA MILANESE (*Via Conca del Naviglio 7, tel 02 58114843, €€€*), served in a pleasantly vintage setting.

DAY 2

❶ Castello Sforzesco (see pp. 154–155) Explore the many museums within this well-known Milanese landmark, once a military fortress and home to the mighty Sforza family. Should you need to get outside, exit past the Pietà exhibit straight into the green of ■ PARCO SEMPIONE (see p. 26), Milan's Central Park.

❷ Triennale (see pp. 151–152) Near this imposing fascist building, where design-themed exhibits are regularly held, rises ■ TORRE BRANCA (see pp. 152–153), Milan's first TV tower, opened in 1933. In 90 seconds the elevator will take you to the viewing platform 325 feet (99 m) high, where you will have the city at your feet. At its base, ■ JUST CAVALLI RESTAURANT & CLUB (*Via Luigi Camoens, tel 02 311817, €€€€€*) is open in the evenings as a restaurant and from 11 p.m. as a club. Less formal, but still in verdant Parco Sempione, ■ BAR BIANCO (*Viale Ibsen 4, tel 02 86992926, €€*) is open all day. It is a particularly popular spot for *aperitivi* in summer.

❸ Pinacoteca di Brera (see pp. 106–107) In the charming Brera neighborhood, heart of Milan's artistic community for centuries, you'll find Palazzo di Brera, housing the famous Pinacoteca, the Academy of Fine Arts, and the ■ BIBLIOTECA NAZIONALE

SAVVY **TRAVELER**

Milan shows its cultural and contemporary vibe through its festivals, when the town buzzes with international visitors. Milan Design Week sparks **Fuorisalone** (*fuorisalone.it*) in April; May brings **Piano City,** when pianists perform public concerts in their homes; and with the month of September comes the street party, **Vogue Fashion Night Out.**

BRAIDENSE (*Via Brera 28, tel 02 86460907, closed Sun.*). In addition to its many rare volumes, this library showcases Milanese book production. In the same complex is pretty ■ ORTO BOTANICO DI BRERA (*tel 02 50314680*), a tiny botanical garden that is perfect for a museum break. Nearby is ■ CUBO BOOKSHOP & CAFFETTERIA DEGLI ATELLANI (*Via della Moscova 28, tel 02 36535957, atellani.it*), in a modern glass structure. Don't miss the ■ MUSEO DEL RISORGIMENTO (*Via Borgonuovo 23, tel 02 88448135, closed Mon.*), close by in the 18th-century Moriggia Palace.

❹ Fashion District (see pp. 50–51)

❺ Poldi Pezzoli (see p. 58) If museums in historic houses excite you, head to the nearby ■ MUSEO BAGATTI VALSECCHI (see p. 34). With the Poldi Pezzoli, Villa Necchi Campiglio (see p. 74), and Casa Boschi di Stefano (see pp. 64–65), it is part of the ■ CIRCUIT OF THE MUSEUM HOUSES OF MILAN (*casemuseomilano.it*).

Milan for Fun

Innovative exhibits, opulent lunch options, and a changing city, ending with new venues of Milan's nightlife.

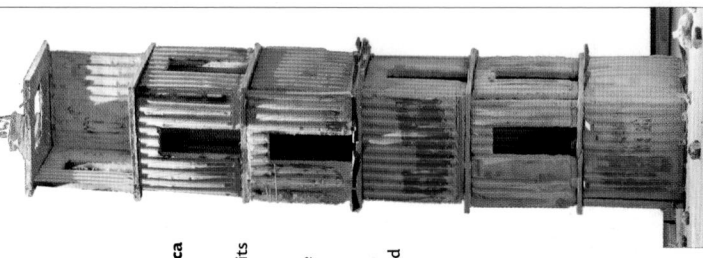

7 Hangar Bicocca (see p. 126)
Surprising and site-specific exhibits await within the former Ansaldo-Breda factory. The three evening openings are a big plus. Head back to Isola for dinner and late-night fun.

6 Isola Garibaldi
There is everything to discover in this old neighborhood that has become the new frontier of Milan's alternative nightlife. For a weekend night visit, take Metro Line 5 for five stops to Ponale, then follow Via Chiese on your left.

5 Piazza Gae Aulenti (see p. 104)
This large new public space was the centerpiece of the Expo 2015 renovation of Milan's skyline. From here it is a short walk to Isola following the pedestrian walkway past the two Bosco Verticale buildings, then left on Via Confalonieri and right on Via Borsieri, Isola's main drag.

VIA CONFALONIERI

Hangar Bicocca

VIA P. BORSIERI

Isola Garibaldi 6

7

Stazione Porta Garibaldi

VIA LUIGI STURZO

PIAZZA GAE AULENTI 5

VIALE

VIA FRAT. CASTIGLIONI

VIA CARLO DE CRISTOFORIS

PIAZZA XXV APRILE

VIA MONTE GRAPPA

BASTIONI DI PORTA NUOVA

Eataly Smeraldo 4

VIA CASTELFIDARDO

VIA PASUBIO

VIALE FRANCESCO CRISPI

VIA VARESE

VIA VOLTA

CORSO GARIBALDI

VIA MARSALA

VIA STATUTO

VIA SOLFERINO

VIA

DELLA MOSCOVA

4 Eataly Smeraldo (see p. 101) Satisfying the eyes as well as the palate, this huge space is devoted to the pleasures of eating and thus a perfect lunch stop. After, follow Corso Como until you see some skyscrapers on your right, then take the escalator to Piazza Gae Aulenti.

3 Parco Sempione Stretch your legs in Milan's very own version of Central Park, at the back of Castello Sforzesco. Then follow Corso Garibaldi all the way to Eataly.

2 Brera (see pp. 97–107) Enjoy the pleasure of wandering aimlessly through the narrow cobbled streets of this artsy district, now largely pedestrian only. A short walk down Via Pontaccio and Via Rivoli leads to the park.

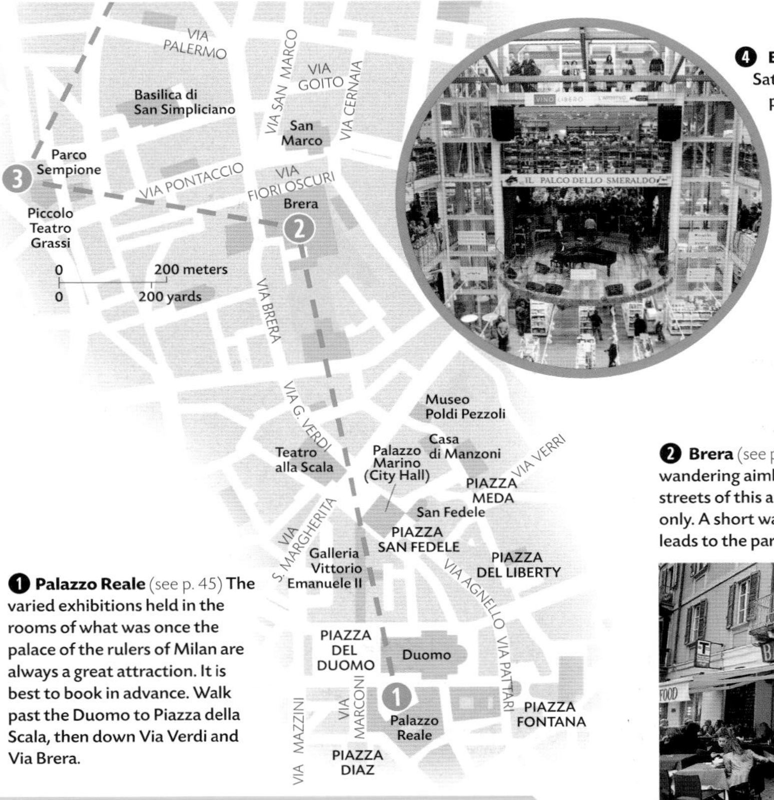

1 Palazzo Reale (see p. 45) The varied exhibitions held in the rooms of what was once the palace of the rulers of Milan are always a great attraction. It is best to book in advance. Walk past the Duomo to Piazza della Scala, then down Via Verdi and Via Brera.

MILAN FOR FUN DISTANCE: 6.6 MILES (10.6 KM)
TIME: ABOUT 8 HOURS METRO START: DUOMO, LINE 1

Map labels:

VIA PALERMO · VIA SAN MARCO · VIA GOITO · VIA CERNAIA · Basilica di San Simpliciano · VIA PONTACCIO · San Marco · VIA FIORI OSCURI · Brera · Parco Sempione · Piccolo Teatro Grassi · 200 meters · 200 yards · VIA BRERA · VIA G. VERDI · Teatro alla Scala · Museo Poldi Pezzoli · Casa di Manzoni · VIA VERRI · PIAZZA MEDA · Palazzo Marino (City Hall) · San Fedele · PIAZZA SAN FEDELE · PIAZZA DEL LIBERTY · VIA DEL AGNELLO · VIA PATTARI · Galleria Vittorio Emanuele II · VIA MARGHERITA · PIAZZA DEL DUOMO · Duomo · Palazzo Reale · PIAZZA DIAZ · VIA MARCONI · VIA MAZZINI · PIAZZA FONTANA

Palazzo Reale

1 This once opulent neoclassical palace next to the cathedral is the favored location for the most important exhibitions in Milan and it always attracts a large number of visitors. To avoid waiting in line, book in advance (see p. 45).

Piazza del Duomo 12 • tel 02 88445181 • viscontisforza.it • Closed Mon. a.m. • €€€ • Metro: Duomo, Line 1, 3 • Tram: 2, 14, 15, 16, 24, 27

GOOD **EATS**

■ **ALICE**

The restaurant Alice is run by Viviana Varese, a starred chef with a passion for fish that is expertly chosen by Sandra Ciciriello, who is also the sommelier. Located on the second floor of Eataly overlooking Piazza XXV Aprile. **Piazza XXV Aprile 10, tel 02 49497430, aliceristorante.it, closed Sun., €€€€€**

■ **PARMA & CO**

Culatello, Parma ham, cappelletti, ravioli, and *gnocco fritto*–the best of Parma cuisine may be found in this venue with a twin soul, as it is both a delicatessen and a restaurant known for its tastings and Sunday brunch. **Via Tessa 2 near Corso Garibaldi, tel 02 89096720, €€€**

■ **RATANÀ**

From the early 20th-century building surrounded by new Porta Nuova skyscrapers to the menu selection, it is clear that tradition is important to chef Cesare Battisti. Here you will find all the classics of Lombard cuisine, but in lighter versions with a modern touch. At aperitif time enjoy the delicious *rubitt,* bite-size delicacies that are a Milanese version of tapas. **Via de Castillia 28, tel 02 87128855, closed Mon.–Tues., €€€€**

Brera

2 Between Piazza del Carmine and Piazza San Marco, the region of Brera is a reminder of old Milan. While the neighborhood has undergone change, you can still stop at **Jamaica** (*Via Brera 32, tel 02 876723, €€*), from early morning to late night. This eatery has long been a spot for intellectuals and artists in this most bohemian area of the city.

Parco Sempione

3 Filled with trees, flowers, and sculptures, this is Milan's largest park in the city center, stretching all the way from the back of Castello Sforzesco to Arco della Pace. Two scenic picnic spots are the Laghetto, a small lake, and the romantic Ponte delle Sirenette, a bridge decorated with mermaid statues.

Eataly Smeraldo

4 Buy, eat, and learn: These are the three basic principles of Eataly Smeraldo, a perfect stop to gather picnic items or enjoy a sit-down meal. The three enormous floors devoted to the pleasures of food include thirteen themed restaurants, five areas for food made on-site—from mozzarella to pasta— and a starred restaurant, **Alice** (see sidebar this page).

Piazza XXV Aprile 10 • tel 02 49497301 • eataly.it • Metro: Moscova, Line 2; Garibaldi F. S., Line 2, 5 • Bus: 94

Piazza Gae Aulenti

5 In a city with fairly few piazzas, this striking new space in the Porta Nuova neighborhood was designed by the Argentine architect Cesar Pelli, who was also responsible for the sleek adjacent UniCredit Tower. It has quickly become a favorite Milanese meeting point. The round piazza, 262 feet (80 m) in diameter, is punctuated by three fountains and an installation by Alberto Garutti (see p. 104). In addition to admiring the architecture, people come here for a **Grom** gelato or to browse the varied selection of **Feltrinelli Red,** a bookstore that is also open in the evenings as a literary stop for those strolling beneath the lit-up high-rises.

Metro: Garibaldi F. S., Line 2, 5

Isola Garibaldi

6 The Isola neighborhood has kept its old popular charm while acquiring an alternative character, becoming in just a few years one of the most vibrant corners of Milan's nightlife. Among the most popular places for *aperitivi* and dinner is the **Deus Café** *(Via Thaon de Revel 3, tel 02 83439230, deuscafe.it, €€€),* attached to a motorcycle shop, while music lovers enjoy the casual atmosphere and live music of the **Nordest Caffè** *(Via Borsieri 35, tel 02 69001910, €€).* To end the evening you can choose between **Alcatraz** *(Via Valtellina 25, tel 02 69016352),* which alternates weeknight concert gigs with weekend dance nights, and the clubs of Corso Como and its surroundings, starting with the famous **Hollywood** *(no. 10, tel 02 6598996).*

Metro: Isola, Line 5; Garibaldi F. S., Line 2, 5

Hangar Bicocca

7 The exhibitions of contemporary art in this converted factory space are always large-scale international events, with site-specific projects such as "**The Seven Heavenly Palaces**" by Anselm Kiefer, created for the opening of the hangar and now part of the permanent exhibition. Evening openings are particularly popular. For a stylish dinner, book a table at its innovative on-site restaurant **Dopolavoro Bicocca** *(tel 02 6431111, closed Mon.–Tues.).*

Via Chiese 2 • tel 02 66111573 • hangarbicocca.org • Closed Mon.–Wed. • Bus: 51, 87, 728

Milan With Kids

View Milan surrounded by sculptured saints, inspect ancient swords and armor, and go inside a real submarine on this full day with the family.

❺ Museo Nazionale della Scienza e della Tecnologia (see pp. 136–137) There's an abundance of intriguing exhibits in this converted monastery. Wearing a safety helmet, you can go inside the *Enrico Toti* submarine and explore its airtight chambers, echolocation equipment, and engine room. Just remember to book in advance.

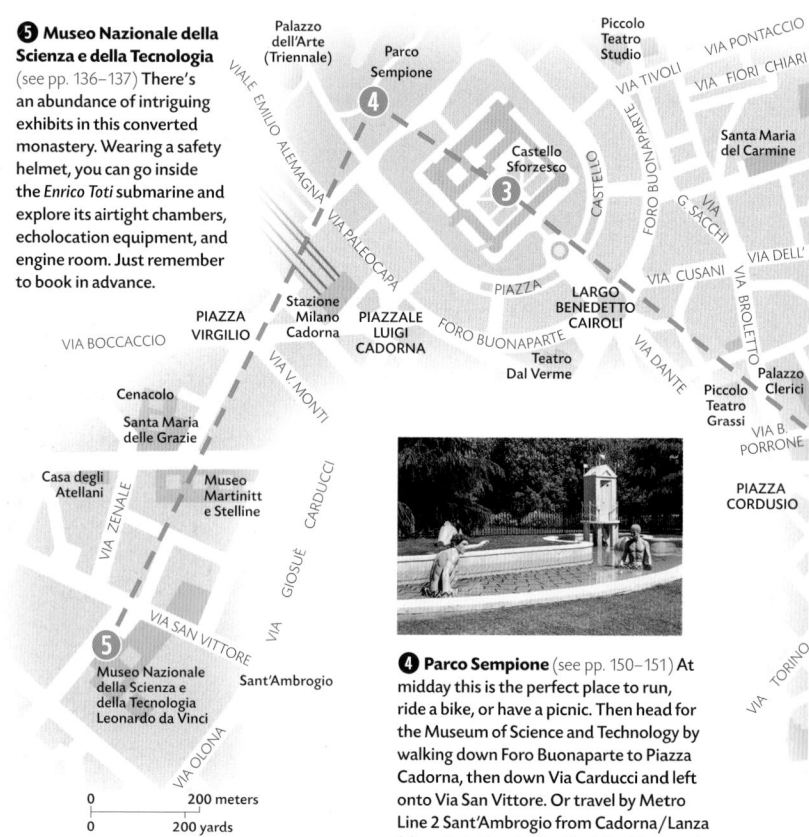

❹ Parco Sempione (see pp. 150–151) At midday this is the perfect place to run, ride a bike, or have a picnic. Then head for the Museum of Science and Technology by walking down Foro Buonaparte to Piazza Cadorna, then down Via Carducci and left onto Via San Vittore. Or travel by Metro Line 2 Sant'Ambrogio from Cadorna/Lanza (closest stations to the Castello Sforzesco).

**MILAN WITH KIDS   DISTANCE: 2.5 MILES (4 KM)
TIME: ABOUT 6 HOURS   METRO START: PORTA ROMANA, LINE 3**

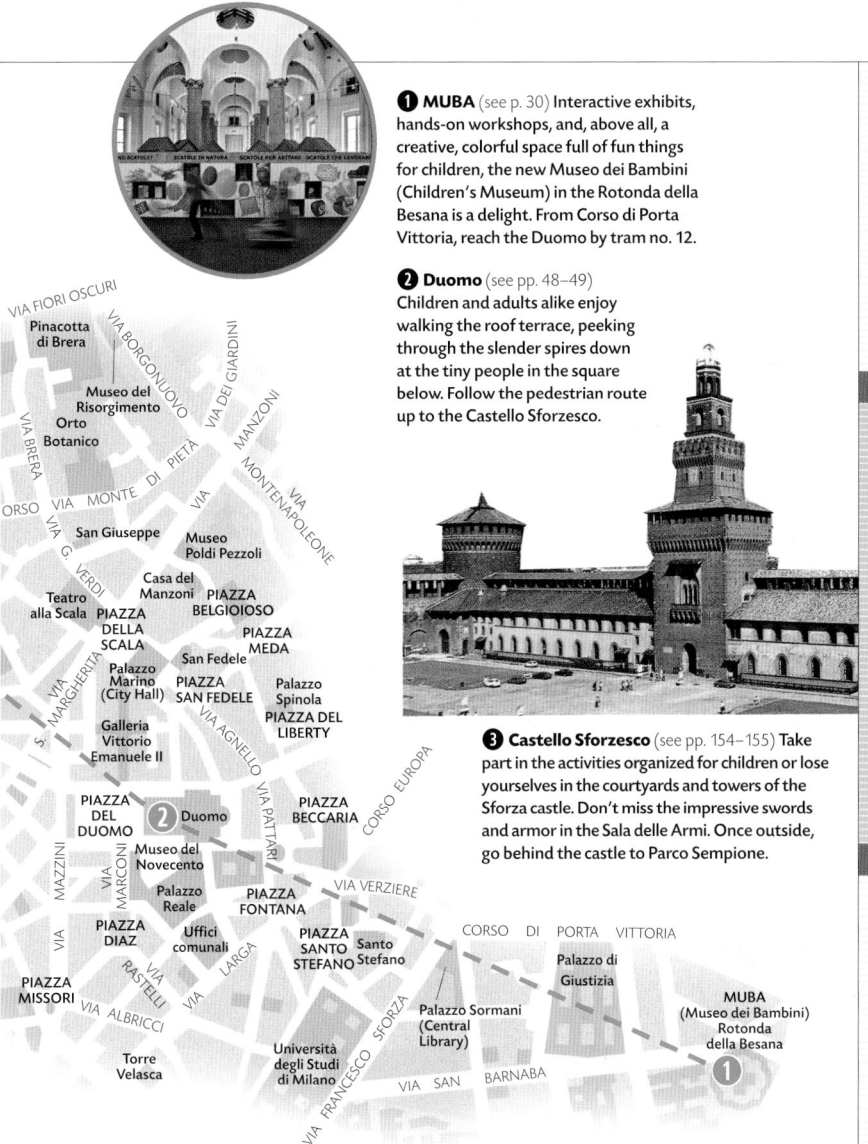

❶ MUBA (see p. 30) Interactive exhibits, hands-on workshops, and, above all, a creative, colorful space full of fun things for children, the new Museo dei Bambini (Children's Museum) in the Rotonda della Besana is a delight. From Corso di Porta Vittoria, reach the Duomo by tram no. 12.

❷ Duomo (see pp. 48–49) Children and adults alike enjoy walking the roof terrace, peeking through the slender spires down at the tiny people in the square below. Follow the pedestrian route up to the Castello Sforzesco.

❸ Castello Sforzesco (see pp. 154–155) Take part in the activities organized for children or lose yourselves in the courtyards and towers of the Sforza castle. Don't miss the impressive swords and armor in the Sala delle Armi. Once outside, go behind the castle to Parco Sempione.

MUBA

1 MUBA, the Museo dei Bambini (Children's Museum), organizes interactive exhibits and workshops with the goal of combining learning and play. In 2014 it found a wonderful permanent home in the octagonal **Rotonda della Besana** (see p. 86), a beautiful colonnaded building with a large enclosed garden, ideal for children to play in.

Via Besana 12 • tel 02 43980402 • muba.it • €€€ • Bus: 73, 77, 84 • Tram: 9, 12, 23, 27

Duomo

2 This is an essential stop for anyone visiting the city. Children will especially enjoy going up to the **roof terrace,** either on foot (257 steps) or by the elevator. From here, there is a magnificent view of the entire city. It is also fun to have a close-up view of the forest of **spires and statues** (more than 1,800 in all) that populate the cathedral roof.

Piazza del Duomo • tel 02 72022656 • duomomilano.it • Museo closed Mon. • Elevator €€€, reduced €€, by foot €€, reduced € • Metro: Duomo, Line 1, 3 • Tram: 2, 14, 15, 16, 24, 27

Guided tours of six people at a time explore the *Enrico Toti* submarine, launched in 1967 and decommissioned in 1999, now beached at the Museo della Scienza e della Tecnologia.

Castello Sforzesco

3 This castle with its towers and moats is in itself a great place for children to explore and run around in, but for ages 4 to 11, the place to be is **Sforzinda,** a play and discovery area in the inner moat of the Piazza d'Armi. Also entertaining are guided tours to the **Museum of Musical Instruments.**

Piazza Castello–Piazza d'Armi • tel 02 88463700 • milanocastello.it • Activities for families on Sun., school holidays • € • Metro: Cadorna, Cairoli, Line 1; Cadorna, Lanza, Line 2 • Bus: 18, 50, 57, 58, 61, 94 • Tram: 1, 2, 4, 12, 14, 19

Parco Sempione

4 Sempione Park, Milan's equivalent of Central Park, was laid out in the English landscape style in 1890 with great swaths for running out excess energy as well as relaxing over a picnic. Children in particular enjoy the playground, skating rink, and **Aquarium.** You can also take part in one of the activities organized by TDMKids (*Viale Alemagna 6, tel 02 72434208*), the educational arm of the **Triennale Design Museum** (see pp. 151–152), introducing design to children ages three to ten.

Museo della Scienza e della Tecnologia

5 There's loads for kids to explore in this museum of science and technology: a real tall ship, Leonardo's designs executed in wooden models, and imaginative themed exhibits. One highlight is the *Enrico Toti* **submarine:** By booking well in advance, children over the age of three can have the amazing experience of going on board via a 20-minute guided tour.

Via San Vittore 21 • tel 02 485551 • museoscienza.org • Museum entrance and guided tour • Closed Mon. • €€€ • Metro: Sant'Ambrogio, Line 2 • Bus: 50, 58, 94

GOOD **EATS**

■ PANINO GIUSTO
The first shop of what would later become an international chain opened here more than 30 years ago. It has remained faithful to its origins, meaning here you can still eat the tastiest panini (filled rolls) in Milan. **Corso Garibaldi 125, tel 02 6554728, €€**

■ PIZZERIA SPONTINI
People have been coming to this eatery for a slice of delicious pizza since the 1950s. The recipe has not changed over the years: a soft and crisp base, with tomato, oregano, anchovies, and mozzarella cheese. **Via Santa Radegonda 11 near the Duomo (5 more locations in the city), tel 02 89092621, €**

■ ROTONDA BISTRO
Located at MUBA in the Rotonda della Besana, this café and restaurant includes a pleasant outdoor terrace. Local products and ingredients are used and there are special dishes for children. **Via Besana 12, tel 02 55011404, closed Mon., €€**

WHIRLWIND TOURS

Shopping in Milan

Famous fashion names and unique items, vintage clothes and streetwear: The window displays change with the district.

❸ Brera and Garibaldi
Boutiques, vintage shops, and concept stores (see pp. 110–111) make the Brera quarter a unique experience. Take Metro Line 2 from Garibaldi three stops to Cadorna; walk down Via Carducci and turn left on Corso Magenta.

❹ Magenta and Its Surroundings The Cinque Vie (Five Streets) district and the fashionable shops of the Corso Magenta are the Milanese equivalent of the Marais in Paris. Elegant boutiques and shops featuring high-end craftsmanship abound. For a different look, follow Via Carducci and Via de Amicis to Corso di Porta Ticinese and Colonne di San Lorenzo.

❺ Ticinese District
Sneakers, sweatshirts, and T-shirts: The hottest streetwear items are to be found on Corso di Porta Ticinese and Via Torino. For quirky and vintage fashion, head the other way on Ticinese toward Navigli.

SHOPPING IN MILAN   DISTANCE: 3 MILES (5 KM)
TIME: ABOUT 8 HOURS   METRO START: PORTA VENEZIA, LINE 1

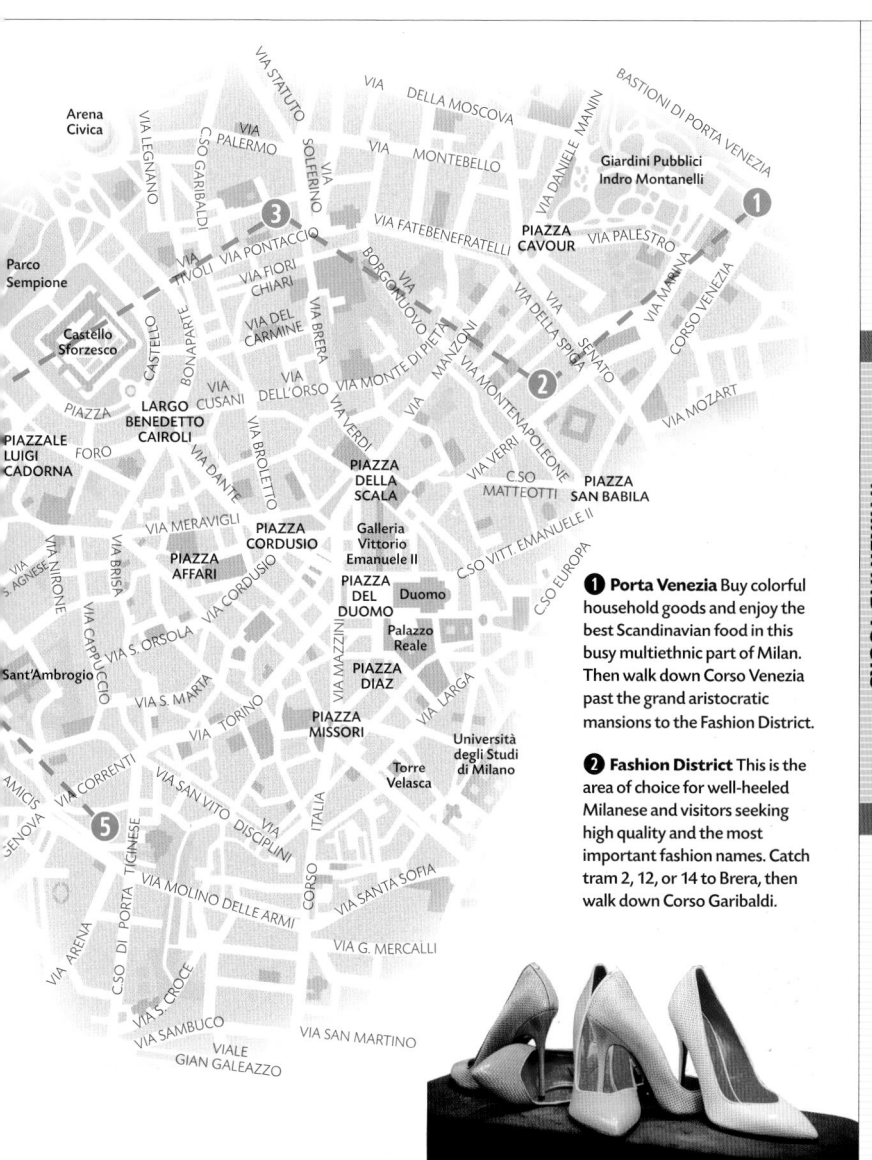

1 Porta Venezia Buy colorful household goods and enjoy the best Scandinavian food in this busy multiethnic part of Milan. Then walk down Corso Venezia past the grand aristocratic mansions to the Fashion District.

2 Fashion District This is the area of choice for well-heeled Milanese and visitors seeking high quality and the most important fashion names. Catch tram 2, 12, or 14 to Brera, then walk down Corso Garibaldi.

WHIRLWIND TOURS

Porta Venezia

1 The element of craftmanship is prominent in the shop windows of this popular neighborhood. For example, in her shop in part of a renovated former 17th-century convent, **Lisa Corti** (*Via Lecco 2*) presents cheerful, colorful collections of clothes and items for the home, inspired by India. A Swedish-themed store with sleek design, all light-colored wood and clean surfaces, **Björk Side Store** (*Via Panfilo Castaldi 20*) has a delicatessen selling Swedish food as well as an interesting selection of modern and older Scandinavian objects. Irony and a light touch are the marks of the funky **Carpe Diem** (*Viale Tunisia 1*), a shop selling highly original furniture and other objects that make fun presents.

Metro: Porta Venezia, Line 1; Repubblica, Line 3

Fashion District

2 Dubbed Quadrilatero d'Oro, or "rectangle of gold"—as well as Quadrilatero della Moda ("fashion")—here you will find the major pricey Italian and international fashion labels (see pp. 50–51), and also established shops such as **Vetrerie di Empoli** (*Via Montenapoleone 22*), a kingdom of crystal goblets and other glassware as well as fine china. Eclectic objects and designer items are to be found in Rossana Orlandi's original shop in the **Bagatti Valsecchi Museum** (*Via Gesù 5*). One address that has changed with the times is the **Nella Longari Home** (*Via Bigli 12*), offering two floors of shopping for household articles and accessories ranging from the classic to the contemporary.

Metro: San Babila, Line 1; Montenapoleone, Line 3

A vision in red at the Valentino store on Via Montenapoleone

Brera and Garibaldi

3 Unique pieces, sophisticated boutiques, and an authentic Milanese atmosphere all combine to make this area an irresistible shopping experience. For fashion lovers, the focus is **Antonia** (*Via Cusani 5*), a multibrand boutique offering the best of Italian and foreign collections for both sexes. Recently opened in

Milan, the cult brand **L'Autre Chose** *(Via Fiori Chiari 16)* blends retro and contemporary styles. The finest linen, including in particular *froissée,* or creased linen, can be bought at **Society** *(Via Palermo 1)*. For wine lovers, **N'Ombra de Vin** (see pp. 52–53; *Via San Marco 2)* is a classic wine bar and meeting place for an *aperitivo*. If you covet notebooks, pencils, paper, and original cards, do not miss **Rigadritto** *(Via Brera 6)*.

Metro: Moscova and Lanza, Line 2; Montenapoleone, Line 3

Magenta and Its Surroundings

4 Creativity in excellent taste is easily found here. Well worth a visit is the concept store **Wait and See** (see p. 111), as well as **Pellini,** a sophisticated jewelry studio with two shops in the area *(Via Morigi 9 & Corso Magenta 11)*. Still on Corso Magenta, **Pérfume by Calé** *(no. 22)* presents the creations of great perfumery artists in a modern environment, with classic fragrances and new scents side by side. Book lovers and design buffs flock to **Bookstore of the Triennale** *(Viale Alemagna 6)*, where books on architecture, design, and modern and contemporary art are shelved alongside gadgets and other interesting items.

Ticinese District

5 Among the large clothing store chains on Via Torino and its surroundings, streetwear is running wild, starting with **Treesse** *(no. 18)*, where you can find the very best in sneakers, sweatshirts, and T-shirts. Along nearby Via de Amicis is the home of hip-hop clothing, **Wag** *(no. 28)*, a showcase of urban culture. If you're seeking sneakers, especially limited editions, head over to Corso di Porta Ticinese, where **Par 5** *(no. 16)* and **Special** *(no. 80)* will outfit your feet.

Metro: Duomo, Line 1, 3; Sant'Ambrogio, Line 2

GOOD **EATS**

■ **ALBUFERA**
Here new Spanish tapas preserve authentic flavors. Also excellent are the classic Valencian paella and the traditional *fideuá,* paella made with pasta. **Via Lecco 15, tel 02 36686993, closed Mon., €€€**

■ **BICE**
A favorite of designers, actors, and musicians who appreciate the authentic flavors of traditional Tuscan cuisine, from *ribollita* soup to chestnut cake, as well as some Milanese dishes such as risotto with osso buco. **Via Borgospesso 12, tel 02 76002572, closed Mon., €€€€€**

■ **CAPRA E CAVOLI**
Focusing on vegetarian food (with a few meat and fish dishes), Chef Barbara Ferrario's inventive menu includes such fare as Risotto non Risotto, made with celeriac instead of rice, and an array of mouthwatering desserts. The decor recalls a secret garden, with mismatched furniture and plants between the tables. **Via Pastrengo 28, tel 02 87066093, closed Sun. p.m.–Mon., €€€**

PART 2

Milan's Neighborhoods

Milan's Neighborhoods

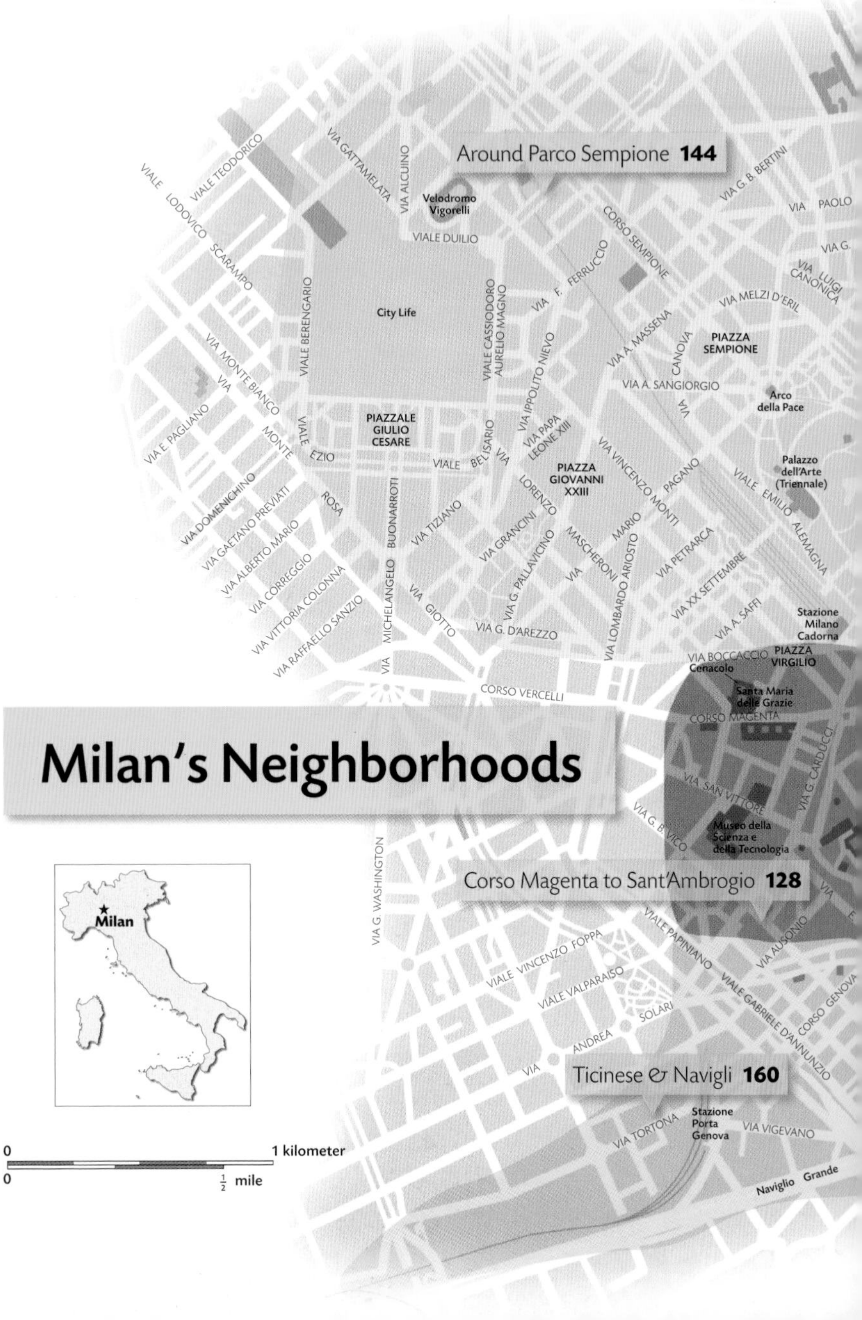

Velodromo Vigorelli

VIALE DUILIO

City Life

PIAZZA SEMPIONE

Arco della Pace

Palazzo dell'Arte (Triennale)

PIAZZALE GIULIO CESARE

PIAZZA GIOVANNI XXIII

Stazione Milano Cadorna

PIAZZA VIRGILIO

Cenacolo

Santa Maria delle Grazie

CORSO MAGENTA

Museo della Scienza e della Tecnologia

Stazione Porta Genova

Naviglio Grande

VIALE LODOVICO SCARAMPO

VIALE TEODORICO

VIA GATTAMELATA

VIA ALCUINO

CORSO SEMPIONE

VIA G. B. BERTINI

VIA PAOLO

VIA G.

VIA LUIGI CANONICA

VIA MELZI D'ERIL

VIALE BERENGARIO

VIALE CASSIODORO AURELIO MAGNO

VIA F. FERRUCCIO

VIA A. MASSENA

CANOVA

VIA A. SANGIORGIO

VIA MONTE BIANCO

VIA

VIALE EZIO

MONTE

VIA IPPOLITO NIEVO

VIA PAPA LEONE XIII

VIA VINCENZO MONTI

PAGANO

VIALE EMILIO ALEMAGNA

VIA E. PAGLIANO

VIALE BELISARIO

VIA BUONARROTI

LORENZO

PIAZZA

VIA PETRARCA

VIA DOMENICHINO

ROSA

VIA TIZIANO

VIA GRANCINI

MASCHERONI

MARIO

VIA XX SETTEMBRE

VIA A. SAFFI

VIA GAETANO PREVIATI

VIA ALBERTO MARIO

VIA CORREGGIO

VIA MICHELANGELO

VIA G. PALLAVICINO

VIA LOMBARDO ARIOSTO

VIA BOCCACCIO

VIA VITTORIA COLONNA

VIA GIOTTO

VIA D'AREZZO

VIA RAFFAELLO SANZIO

CORSO VERCELLI

VIA SAN VITTORE

VIA G. B. VICO

VIA G. CARDUCCI

VIA G. WASHINGTON

VIALE VINCENZO FOPPA

VIALE PAPINIANO

VIA AUGUSTO

VIA E.

VIALE VALPARAISO

VIALE GABRIELE D'ANNUNZIO

CORSO GENOVA

ANDREA

SOLARI

VIA

VIA TORTONA

VIA VIGEVANO

★ **Milan**

0   1 kilometer

0        $\frac{1}{2}$ mile

Cimitero Monumentale

Stazione Porta Garibaldi

PIAZZA GAE AULENTI

Brera & Garibaldi 96

Stazione Centrale

Porta Nuova

PIAZZA DELLA REPUBBLICA

PIAZZALE BIANCAMANO

Arena Civica

Parco Sempione

Giardini Indro Montanelli

PIAZZA CAVOUR

Brera

Castello Sforzesco

Around the Giardini Pubblici 68

PIAZZALE LUIGI CADORNA

LARGO BENEDETTO CAIROLI

PIAZZA DEL TRICOLORE

La Scala & Around 54

Teatro alla Scala

Palazzo Marino (City Hall)

PIAZZA SAN BABILA

Borsa

PIAZZA AFFARI

PIAZZA CORDUSIO

Galleria Vittorio Emanuele II

San Babila to the Galleria 40

PIAZZA DEL DUOMO

Duomo

Pinacoteca Ambrosiana

Palazzo Reale

Basilica di Sant'Ambrogio

Torre Velasca to Piazza Affari 112

Università degli Studi di Milano

Torre Velasca

Palazzo di Giustizia

Rotonda della Besana

Ospedale Maggiore Policlinico

Southeast Milan 82

Darsena

Santa Maria dei Miracoli

PIAZZA XXIV MAGGIO

PIAZZA MEDAGLIE D'ORO

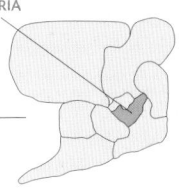

San Babila to the Galleria

This area forms the very heart of the city. It extends from the Piazza San Babila along the pedestrian street of Corso Vittorio Emanuele II to the magnificent Duomo, the Gothic symbol of Milan. On this walk you can linger before the windows of internationally known luxury goods stores, the upscale La Rinascente department store, and the celebrated Fashion District. There are also many interesting buildings to see, including the churches of San Babila and San Carlo al Corso. Culture is also represented in the Piazza del Duomo, with important special exhibitions held in the Palazzo Reale (Royal Palace) and the new Museo del Novecento (Museum of the 20th Century). Behind a sleek fascist-era facade, this museum displays selections from its large collection of Italian and international painting and sculpture from the last century.

◗ **At the heart of the city, Milan's cathedral, or Duomo, is a masterpiece of the flamboyant late Gothic style. It was begun in 1386.**

San Babila to the Galleria

Spend a morning or afternoon enjoying the sacred and the shopping in the center of Milan.

6 Museo del Novecento (see p. 46) Stunning Italian art of the past century is on view in this new museum in the Palazzo dell'Arengario. Cross the square to the pedestrian Via Mercanti; the covered Piazza dei Mercanti is on your left.

7 Piazza dei Mercanti (see p. 46) This, along with the Palazzo della Ragione, is the center of medieval Milan, built in 1233 and also known as the Broletto Nuovo. Retrace your steps to Piazza del Duomo and the Galleria.

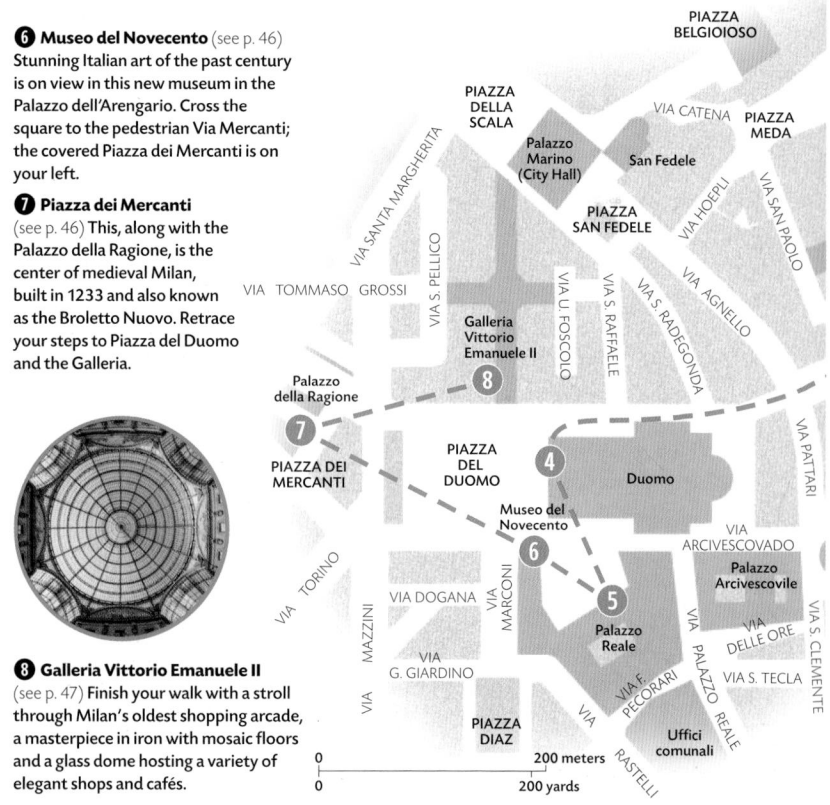

8 Galleria Vittorio Emanuele II (see p. 47) Finish your walk with a stroll through Milan's oldest shopping arcade, a masterpiece in iron with mosaic floors and a glass dome hosting a variety of elegant shops and cafés.

**SAN BABILA TO THE GALLERIA   DISTANCE: 0.6 MILE (1 KM)
TIME: ABOUT 4 HOURS   METRO START: SAN BABILA, LINE 1**

❶ Piazza San Babila (see p. 44)
This is the starting point of the pedestrian area that includes Corso Vittorio Emanuele II, Piazza del Duomo, Via Mercanti, and Via Dante leading to the Castello Sforzesco.

❷ Basilica di San Babila (see p. 44)
Take a look at the restored early 20th-century facade of this ancient church before entering the busy shopping street Corso Vittorio Emanuele II.

❸ Corso Vittorio Emanuele II
(see p. 45) As well as the wares of shops, this street showcases buildings by some of the great architects of the 20th century, including Magistretti, Muzio, and Studio BBPR. Follow it all the way to the Duomo.

❹ Duomo (see pp. 48–49) After taking in the breathtaking exterior, you can admire the sculptures and the beautiful stained-glass windows within. Go up to the roof terraces for a closer look at the golden Madonnina statue and a superb view of the city. Back on street level, look for the Palazzo Reale, set back from the square.

❺ Palazzo Reale (see p. 45)
This former 14th-century ducal palace was rebuilt by Piermarini in the late 18th century. Today it houses the Museo della Reggia, the Museo del Duomo, and the city's most important exhibitions. Museo del Novecento is next door.

Map labels:
VIA VERRI
VIA MONTENAPOLEONE
VIA BAGUTTA
CORSO VENEZIA
CORSO MATTEOTTI
VIA SAN PIETRO ALL'ORTO
Basilica di San Carlo al Corso
Palazzo Spinola
PIAZZA DEL LIBERTY
CORSO VITTORIO EMANUELE II
V. C. BECCARIA
PIAZZA FONTANA
LARGO BERSAGLIERI
LARGO CORSIA DEI SERVI
San Vito
CORSO EUROPA
PIAZZA BECCARIA
Basilica di San Babila
PIAZZA SAN BABILA
LARGO TOSCANINI
Palazzo Durini

Piazza San Babila

1 A century of demolitions, reconstructions, and redesigns transformed a small square into the hub known today as Piazza San Babila, linking Corso Venezia, Corso Matteotti, and Corso Vittorio Emanuele II. Here Milanese gather amid a mishmash of architectural styles—from grand Renaissance palazzi to functional modern buildings from the fascist era to the Romanesque basilica that gives the piazza its name—with one side of the square reserved for pedestrians. A favorite meeting spot is the **fountain** at its center, designed by architect Luigi Caccia Dominioni, which symbolizes the ecosystem of Lombardy with its water and mountain rocks. Just opposite the church rises **Torre Snia Viscosa,** Milan's first skyscraper and tallest building when it was built in 1937; it was then known as *rubanuvole* (cloud thief).

Metro: San Babila, Line 1 • Bus: 54, 60, 61, 73

Basilica di San Babila

2 Like the piazza in which it is set, the Basilica di San Babila has been restored many times, and it provides a welcome quiet place to sit in

the midst of the busy piazza. The church's proximity to the Porta Orientale (Eastern Gate) may have started the legend that the church was built on the ruins of a pagan Temple of the Sun. Today it is an excellent example of reconstruction. The building dates from the 11th century, its current Romanesque appearance the result of a restoration carried out at the end of the 19th century by the architect Cesa Bianchi. Inside, three naves are divided by pillars showing residual traces of frescoes. The **paintings** in the side apses and the **mosaic** in the central one are by Luigi Cavenaghi (1915). Standing in front of the church, the **column of the Lion of the Eastern Gate** marks Venice's failed attempt to conquer Milan.

High above the main entrance of San Babila, a mosaic of Jesus bestows blessings.

Piazza San Babila • tel 02 76002877 • sanbabila.org • Metro: San Babila, Line 1 • Bus: 54, 60, 61, 73

Corso Vittorio Emanuele II

3 At the heart of the large pedestrian area running from Piazza San Babila to the Duomo, Corso Vittorio Emanuele II has been one of the city's main shopping streets since the mid-20th century. Formerly the Corsia dei Servi (Servants' Road), it may be the city's only avenue with such a variety of shops, offering high-end luxury as well as department stores. Perhaps as a result, it is busy day and night with office workers, tourists, and Milanese shopping or strolling around. Set back halfway along the *corso* is the neoclassical **Basilica di San Carlo al Corso,** notable for its dome, which is as wide as the body of the church. It was inspired by the Pantheon in Rome.

Duomo

4 See pp. 48–49.

Piazza del Duomo • tel 02 72022656 • duomomilano.it • Museo closed Mon. • Elevator €€€, reduced €€, by foot €€, reduced € • Metro: Duomo, Line 1, 3 • Tram: 2, 14, 15, 16, 24, 27

Palazzo Reale

5 In the late 18th century, Maria Theresa of Austria ordered the original 14th-century Palazzo Reale (Royal Palace) rebuilt in the neoclassical style by Piermarini, and commissioned various artists to design its sumptuous rooms. These interiors were mainly destroyed by heavy bombing in World War II, but the sweeping staircases, vast halls, and grand art collection of its royal residents remain. Today the site is renowned for its spectacular temporary **exhibitions,** making it an important destination for art lovers to view modern art, as well as fashion and design shows. Be aware that the Duomo Museum here is different from the one in the cathedral itself, showcasing tapestries and other treasures along with great large-scale models.

Piazza del Duomo 12 • tel 02 88445181 • Closed Mon. a.m. • €€€ • Metro: Duomo, Line 1, 3 • Tram: 2, 14, 15, 16, 24, 27

Museo del Novecento

6 Opened in December 2010, the fresh Museo del Novecento showcases a strong permanent collection of 20th-century Italian and European painting and sculpture. Working within the **Palazzo dell'Arengario** and the second floor of the Palazzo Reale, Italo Rota designed a top-notch museum space where displays form an artistic timeline, starting with "Il Quarto Stato" ("The Fourth Estate") by Giuseppe Pellizza da Volpedo (1898–1902) and ending with Arte Povera, with works of the Futurists, metaphysical painting, Spatialism, and more along the way. For example, a room devoted to the international avant-garde holds works by Picasso, Braque, and Kandinsky. The museum's collection of art by Umberto Boccioni is the finest in the world. And, from room 11, the view of the Duomo is a masterpiece unto itself.

Via Marconi 1 • tel 02 88444061 • museodelnovecento.org • Closed Mon. a.m • €€, free Fri. from 3:30 p.m. • Metro: Duomo, Line 1, 3 • Tram: 2, 14, 15, 16, 24, 27

Piazza dei Mercanti

7 Step back in time to medieval Milan at the Piazza dei Mercanti and the imposing Palazzo della Ragione, built in 1233 as a judicial building and now devoted to photography. Look for the pre-Roman bas-relief on the capital of the second arch depicting the *semilanuta* (half-woolly sow) that, according to legend, showed the Celt Belloveso where to found the city. The palace overlooks the covered **Loggia dei Mercanti** and the **Loggia degli Osii,** two superimposed loggias in white marble with black marble bands. This was the center of city life in the 13th century, when construction of the Duomo hadn't yet begun and

GOOD **EATS**

■ **GIACOMO ARENGARIO**
In the Museo del Novecento there is food for the body as well as for the mind. This classy restaurant has an interesting menu and superb views from within its large loggia overlooking the Duomo and the Galleria Vittorio Emanuele II.
Via Guglielmo Marconi 1, tel 02 72093814, €€€€

■ **IL SALUMAIO**
Set within the splendid Palazzo Bagatti Valsecchi, this historic Montenapoleone delicatessen is now also a restaurant featuring a classic menu. In fine weather look for seats in the the outdoor palace courtyard.
Via Santo Spirito 10, tel 02 76001123, closed Sat.–Sun. lunch, €€€€€

■ **LUINI**
This place is easy to find by the line outside it. Luini's irresistible *panzerotti* (deep-fried filled pastries) have been a classic since World War II, perfect for a substantial snack between tourist attractions.
Via Santa Radegonda 16, tel 02 86461917, closed Sun.–Mon. p.m., €

the Piazza del Duomo was a meadow. It's architecturally different from the rest of the area, and one of the few survivors of the heavy bombings of World War II.

Piazza dei Mercanti 1 • tel 02 0202 • Palazzo closed Mon. a.m. • €€€ • Metro: Duomo, Line 1, 3; Cordusio, Line 1 • Bus: 54 • Tram: 1, 2, 3, 12, 14, 15, 16, 19, 24

Galleria Vittorio Emanuele II

8 It took 353 tons (320 tonnes) of iron to build the framework of the dome of Milan's *salotto* (living room), the Galleria Vittorio Emanuele II. This glass-and-cast-iron arcade was built by Giuseppe Mengoni in 1865 to connect Piazza del Duomo with Piazza della Scala. It took only two years to build the great Latin cross structure that continues to host visitors and the Milanese day and night at its cafés and shops. These include Zucca (better known as **Camparino**) and **Savini,** a traditional after-theater restaurant founded in 1884. Also in evidence are superb bookshops and, with increasing splendor, the boutiques of the big designer labels, from Vuitton to Gucci, Prada to Armani. At the Galleria's center, a dome 154 feet (47 m) high dominates the so-called **Octagon.** Peer up at its vaults to see mosaic murals of Asia, Africa, Europe, and the Americas. Then look down: The floor is decorated with mosaics of the heraldic symbol of Savoy surrounded by the emblems of the cities of Milan, Turin, Florence, and Rome. The Galleria is always open, with two arched entryways on Piazza del Duomo and Piazza della Scala. It's at its most atmospheric in the afternoon and pre-theater time, when the shops are open and the cafés are full of people sipping coffee or *aperitivi.*

A view beneath the great glass dome of the Octagon, heart of the Galleria Vittorio Emanuele II

Metro: Duomo, Line 1, 3 • Tram: 1, 2, 14, 15, 16, 24, 27

Duomo

Milan's cathedral, or Duomo, is among the greatest Gothic buildings in Europe, and contains works of art created over the course of almost 650 years.

The soaring Gothic sanctuary of the Duomo, Milan's spiritual center

The Duomo, or Cathedral of Santa Maria Nascente, was founded in 1386 on the orders of Gian Galeazzo Visconti, Milan's ruler at the time. In addition to providing a superb focal point for the heart of the old city, it is the third largest church in Europe, behind St. Peter's in Rome and the cathedral of Seville, Spain. It took more than 500 years to complete, employing artists, sculptors, and architects from across Europe. The result is a dazzling variety of architectural styles, along with a wealth of statues, stained glass, and other works of art.

THE EXTERIOR

Start with the extravagant exterior, adorned with 135 spires, 2,245 statues, 96 gargoyles, and around half a mile (1 km) of stone tracery. Climb to the terraces for a better view (see sidebar this page). Much of the facade dates from 1813, created on the orders of Napoleon, who was crowned king of Italy here in 1805. The five bronze doors were added between 1840 and 1965.

THE ENTRANCE

Inside, the Duomo is divided into five aisles supported by 52 pillars, one for each week. On the floor near the entrance is the world's largest sundial (1768), so accurate that it was used for centuries to set the city's clocks. Look for the strip of bronze in the floor, placed so that a ray of sunlight strikes it on June 21, the summer solstice. Stairs to the left lead to the remains of earlier churches on the site.

THE INTERIOR

Move down the right wall, where the first five chapels contain some of the cathedral's best stained glass, which is among the most extensive in Europe

IN **THE KNOW**

Be sure to ascend to the Duomo's roof terraces to walk among the bristling spires and buttresses as you enjoy views of Milan and the Alps beyond. Look for the famous Madonnina (1774), the gilded copper statue of the Virgin at the top of the tallest spire, and the city's highest point until 1958. To reach the terraces you can take an elevator or walk up the 257 steps.

(55 windows in total, depicting 3,600 scenes). Other highlights include the macabre 1562 statue in the right transept of St. Bartholomew clutching his skin (he was martyred by being flayed alive); a three-tiered sculpture (1614) in the choir of St. Ambrose and two Milanese bishops; and the great bronze candelabra (in part 12th century) in the left transept.

GRANDE MUSEO DEL DUOMO

This museum, part of the Palazzo Reale next door, preserves sculptures, paintings, stained glass, and tapestries removed from the Duomo over the years for safekeeping. Highlights include an immense painting by Tintoretto and two models of the Duomo, one in Legos.

Piazza del Duomo • tel 02 72022656 • duomomilano.it • Museo closed Mon. • Ticket offices: Piazza del Duomo, right side; Duomo Info Point, Via Arcivescovado 1; Museo, Piazza del Duomo 12 • Duomo free; combined ticket museum & terraces €€€; terraces €€€ with elevator, €€ on foot • Metro: Duomo, Line 1, 3 • Bus: 54 • Tram: 1, 2, 3, 12, 14

Fashion

Milan came late to the business of fashion *(la moda),* lingering behind Paris and New York, and second best in Italy behind Florence. Then the emergence of three key designers in the 1970s saw Milan propelled to the forefront of a worldwide industry. Today the city plays host to numerous designers, ateliers, and some of Europe's finest fashion stores.

A shop window on Via della Spiga in the Fashion District

The Psychedelic Sixties

One of Milan's earliest fashion pioneers was Elio Fiorucci, born in the city in 1935, whose flamboyant and brightly colored clothes were inspired by the pop art and psychedelic culture of the sixties. After a visit to London in 1965, he opened his first store in Milan in 1967. A large store in New York, opened in 1976, introduced the brand to an eager American audience.

Homegrown Talent

For decades Italy's fashion world centered largely on Florence, and it was here, in one of the city's annual fashion shows, that Milan-based designer Gianni Versace first came to prominence, in the early 1970s. At about the same time, a former Milanese architect, Gianfranco Ferré, also began to design simple but beautifully made clothes. As did a third designer, a dropout medical student and former window dresser named Giorgio Armani. Between 1975 and 1978, all three started their businesses here. In 1975 the city held its first Fashion Week, and in time other designers and established textile manufacturers based in and around the city began to prosper.

New Wave, Old Wave

During the 1980s the city's fashion business went from strength to strength. Designers such as Franco Moschino, Romeo Gigli, Domenico Dolce, and Stefano Gabbana built on the extravagant and often daring styles of Versace and Fiorucci. In 1978 Miuccia Prada revitalized a leather goods company founded by her grandfather in 1913, and by the 1990s Prada (and its stablemate, Miu Miu) had joined Armani as the creative and commercial champions of the more minimalist aesthetic for which Milanese fashion is often known. Today, stores selling the clothes, accessories, and homewares of these and other designers are found across the city, but especially in the so-called Quadrilatero della Moda, or Fashion District, the area bounded by Via Montenapoleone, Via Manzoni, Via della Spiga, and Corso Venezia.

SALES SEASON

During the sales seasons you can find real bargains in the Quadrilatero della Moda (Fashion District). The dates of the twice-yearly sales vary: The winter sales usually start around January 6 and the summer sales begin on the first Saturday in July.

An army of models present Versace's latest collection during Fashion Week.

Gastronomic Shopping

Fabulous high fashion and accessories are not the only things that make Milan one of Italy's great shopping destinations. The city also has a wonderful selection of stores selling food and wine, to enjoy on the spot or pack carefully to take home.

■ TEMPLES TO FOOD

Some stores are a feast for the eyes, never mind the stomach, notably **Peck** *(Via Spadari 9, tel 02 8023161, peck.it)*, founded by a butcher from Prague in 1883 and now a glorious emporium spread over three floors, selling food and wine from Italy and beyond. It stands on a small side street just west of the Duomo. Peck also offers a restaurant and wine bar, plus a café nearby at Via Cesare Cantù 3.

A little east of the Duomo, food fills four floors of the 12-story **Brian & Barry** department store *(Via Durini 28, tel 02 92853304, brianebarry.it)*, opened in 2014. Some of the outlets here are run by Eataly (see p. 26 & sidebar p. 101), an international success story with roots in Turin, in Piedmont. In Milan **Eataly** has a superb collection of artisanal food stores and places to eat under one roof at Piazza XXV Aprile 10. At the other extreme is tiny **Panzerotti Luini** *(Via Santa Redegonda 16, tel 02 86461917, luini.it, closed Sun.)*, just to the north of the cathedral, which dates from 1888. Join the line of office workers waiting to buy the store's *panzerotto,* a pizza-like calzone with different fillings. It's been made from a secret recipe since 1949.

■ WINE

As a city, Milan is obviously not a wine producer. But it lies close to several fine wine regions, notably the Soave region to the east around Lake Garda—known mainly for its white wines—and Franciacorta to the northeast near Lake Iseo, renowned for its sparkling white wines based on Chardonnay, Pinot Noir, and Pinot Blanc grapes.

An excellent place at the heart of the city to taste and buy these and more than 1,000 other wines (and to eat in the downstairs restaurant) is **Signorvino** on the northeast corner of Piazza del Duomo *(Corso Vittorio Emanuele II, tel 02 89092539, signorvino.com).* There's even more choice at **N'Ombra de Vin** *(Via San Marco 2, tel 02 6599650, nombradevin.it),* where 2,500 bottles are kept in the pretty,

SAN BABILA TO THE GALLERIA

The enormous Eataly offers a stomach-growling variety of foodstuffs, as well as restaurants, a cooking school, and places to see chefs in action creating fresh pasta and more.

vaulted cellars of a former 15th-century monastery. Here, too, there is a small café for snacks and to sample wines by the glass.

■ PANETTONE AND PASTRIES

The influence of Milan's erstwhile Austrian occupiers, among other things, means the city is rightly celebrated for its cakes and pastries. Every pastry shop sells panettone, but locals swear by the version made by **Marchesi** *(Via Santa Maria alla Porta 11, tel 02 862770)*. This establishment has had a beautiful shop in the northwest Corso Magenta area since 1824. Interestingly, the famous Prada fashion house recently bought an 80 percent share in the store, allowing it to offer the firm's pastries to patrons at the Fondazione Prada (see p. 127) and its Galleria Vittorio Emanuele menswear store. It is common knowledge that visitors should taste-test at quite a few sweet emporiums before choosing a favorite. One likely destination, a few minutes' walk south of the Duomo near the Missori Metro station, is **Giovanni Galli** *(Corso Porta Romana 2, tel 02 86453112)*. You can choose among many delectable candies and pastries, but be sure to ask for the special marrons glacés, made daily in season from fresh chestnuts.

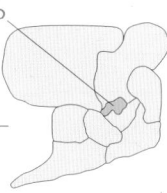

La Scala &
Around

Walking through the neighborhoods north of the Duomo, it is not hard to imagine how Milan looked in the fin-de-siècle days, when Verdi operas serenaded the city and Milan's aristocracy lived in their grandiose palazzi. Here you can visit Alessandro Manzoni's house, close to his beloved church of San Fedele. The composer Giuseppe Verdi lived at the Grand Hotel et de Milan on nearby Via Manzoni, the same street (then known as the Corsia del Giardino) where the young Stendhal was falling in love with the city from his residence in the sumptuous Palazzo Borromeo d'Adda. But the area around La Scala also belongs to the world of banking and finance. Today the Gallerie d'Italia, right next to La Scala, showcases 19th- and 20th-century art owned by Italy's two main banks. It is located in two adjacent 18th-century palazzi, set off by frescoed walls and ceilings.

❍ **Piazza della Scala,
home to perhaps the
most famous opera
house in the world**

La Scala & Around

Wander through the narrow streets of old Milan before enjoying a memorable performance at Teatro alla Scala.

1 San Giuseppe (see p. 58) The little church of San Giuseppe is on Via Verdi, between the 19th-century Ca' de Sass and the Cariplo bank building designed by Greppi and Muzio. Inside is a baroque masterpiece by Francesco Maria Richini. Walk down Via Andegari and Via Romagnosi to the corner of Via Manzoni.

2 Museo Poldi Pezzoli (see p. 58) Gian Giacomo Poldi Pezzoli's house and museum contain an amazingly wide-ranging collection including textiles, weapons, clocks, works by the great Renaissance artists, and stained glass. Head across Via Morone to Casa del Manzoni.

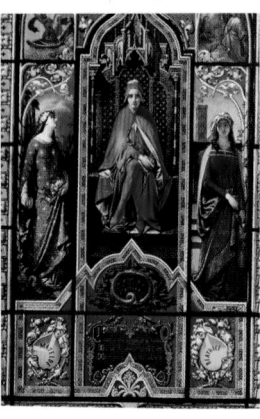

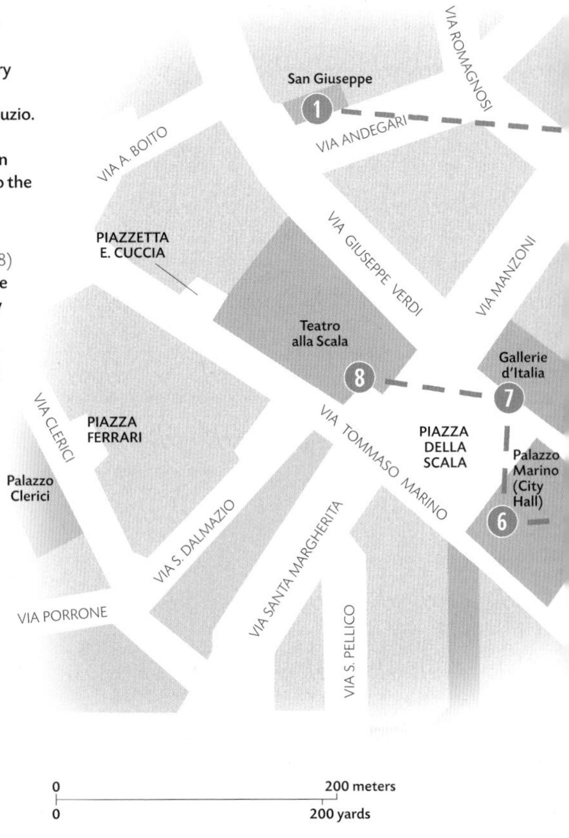
VIA ROMAGNOSI
San Giuseppe
1
VIA ANDEGARI
VIA A. BOITO
PIAZZETTA E. CUCCIA
VIA GIUSEPPE VERDI
VIA MANZONI
Teatro alla Scala
8
Gallerie d'Italia
7
VIA CLERICI
PIAZZA FERRARI
VIA TOMMASO MARINO
PIAZZA DELLA SCALA
Palazzo Marino (City Hall)
Palazzo Clerici
6
VIA S. DALMAZIO
VIA SANTA MARGHERITA
VIA PORRONE
VIA S. PELLICO
0
200 meters
0
200 yards

LA SCALA & AROUND DISTANCE: 0.5 MILE (0.8 KM)
TIME: ABOUT 4 HOURS METRO START: MONTENAPOLEONE, LINE 3

8 Teatro alla Scala (see pp. 62–63) Absorb the neoclassical architecture of Piermarini's building and the history of opera in the Museo Teatrale alla Scala, then enjoy a show.

Museo
Poldi Pezzoli

2

VIA MORONE

Casa del
Manzoni

3

PIAZZA
BELGIOIOSO

Casa degli
Omenoni

4

VIA OMENONI

VIA CATENA

San Fedele

5

PIAZZA
SAN FEDELE

7 Gallerie d'Italia (see p. 61) An extraordinary art collection awaits inside three historic houses, themselves fine examples of Milanese architecture between the 1700s and the early 1900s. The theater is next door.

6 Palazzo Marino (see pp. 60–61) Standing opposite La Scala, this building has been the headquarters of the city council since 1860. Next, cross the Piazza della Scala.

3 Casa del Manzoni (see p. 59) A terra-cotta facade fronts the house where the writer Alessandro Manzoni lived and died, now a museum devoted to his legacy. From Via Morone, walk across Piazza Belgioioso, take a right onto Via Omenoni and look on the right side of the street for no. 3.

4 Casa degli Omenoni (see p. 59) See the eight colossal *atlantes* (figures of men), inspired by Roman statues, on the facade of the palace built by Leone Leoni for himself in the 16th century. Head diagonally across the street toward Piazza San Fedele.

5 San Fedele (see p. 60) Inside this church are works by artists such as Peterzano and Fontana. Walk down Via Tommaso Marino to Piazza della Scala.

San Giuseppe

1 In a piazzetta set back from Via Verdi stands San Giuseppe, the church of St. Joseph, one of the few surviving religious buildings designed by Francesco Maria Richini. Built between 1607 and 1630 on an octagonal plan, it is considered to be his masterpiece and the first fully baroque building in Milan. Next door is the **Palazzo delle Colonne** (Palace of Columns), built between 1937 and 1941, and designed by Giovanni Greppi and Giovanni Muzio to extend the bank building (the former Cassa di Risparmio delle Provincie Lombarde). During World War II, works of art from the Duomo, Brera Gallery, and Biblioteca Ambrosiana were stored in the bank's vaults for safekeeping.

Largo Victor de Sabata • tel 02 8052320 • Metro: Duomo, Line 1, 3

The lovely "Madonna of the Book," by Renaissance artist Sandro Botticelli, hangs in the Museo Poldi Pezzoli.

Museo Poldi Pezzoli

2 For those who love house-museums, this is a gem not to be missed. Founded in 1881 by the collector Gian Giacomo Poldi Pezzoli, it is one of the richest and most interesting private collections in Europe. In addition to the famous **"Portrait of Young Woman"** by Pollaiolo that is its symbol (see p. 6), the museum holds a number of exceptional paintings, including masterpieces by Botticelli, Giovanni Bellini, Mantegna, Piero della Francesca, Tiepolo, and Guardi. Equally important is its **collection of decorative arts:** textiles, porcelain, glass pieces, works of gold, and a whole armory.

Via Manzoni 12 • tel 02 796334 • museopoldipezzoli .it • Closed Tues. • €€€ • Metro: Duomo, Line 1, 3; Montenapoleone, Line 3 • Bus: 61, 94

Casa del Manzoni

3 Alessandro Manzoni, author of plays, poetry, and the beloved novel *I Promessi Sposi (The Betrothed)*, lived in this handsome terra-cotta building on Via Morone from 1813, after his marriage to Enrichetta Blondel, until his death in 1873. Since 1937, the **National Center for Manzonian Studies** has been based here, along with a rich library of books that belonged to the writer and to Stefano Stampa, son of Teresa Borri Stampa, Manzoni's second wife. The **Manzoni Museum** on the first two floors of the building contains original furnishings and books from the writer's bedroom and study, as well as handwritten copies of some of his poems. There are portraits of Manzoni and his family on the walls, along with prints and engravings related to characters and episodes from *The Betrothed,* considered one of the masterpieces of Italian literature. Entrance is free.

Via Morone 1 • tel 02 86460403 • casadelmanzoni.mi.it • Closed Sat.–Mon. • Metro: Duomo, Line 1, 3

Casa degli Omenoni

4 This building takes its name from the eight *atlantes,* figures of Atlas known as *omenoni* (big men) in Milanese dialect, that decorate the facade. They were sculpted by Antonio Abondio, commissioned to create them for the building by his fellow sculptor, Leone Leoni. For many years this was home to an important art collection that included, among other things, the drawings of Leonardo known as the Codex Atlanticus, now preserved in the Biblioteca Ambrosiana (see p. 123). After several changes of ownership, it has been occupied by Clubino, an exclusive gentlemen's club, since 1928. To some, the giants supporting the building now resemble old men, hunched over by the weight of time and a once luxurious past.

Via Omenoni 3 • Metro: Duomo, Line 1, 3

San Fedele

5 A monument to the writer Alessandro Manzoni welcomes visitors to San Fedele. It was erected here in 1883, in front of the church where the beloved author fell and suffered the head injury that led to his death a decade earlier. The 16th-century San Fedele itself is a prototype of the religious architecture of the Counter-Reformation: a central nave with side chapels. In the 18th century the canons of the church of Santa Maria alla Scala, demolished to make room for the Teatro alla Scala, moved to San Fedele with numerous works of art, including the **"Deposition of Christ"** by Simone Peterzano, who taught Caravaggio. The **stations of the cross** and the bas-relief depicting the apparition of the Sacred Heart at Santa Margherita are both ceramic works by Lucio Fontana.

Piazza San Fedele 4 • tel 02 86352215 • Metro: Duomo, Line 1, 3

Palazzo Marino

6 This palace has been the headquarters of Milan's city government since 1861. It was built by the architect Galeazzo Alessi for the rich Genoese merchant Tommaso Marino in the mid-16th century. Originally the main facade was on Piazza San Fedele; the current front, on Piazza della Scala, is the result of 19th-century restoration work by Luca Beltrami. Only occasionally open to visitors, Palazzo Marino has, for the past few years, been displaying masterpieces of Italian art (from Canova to Caravaggio, from Leonardo to Raphael) in the **Sala Alessi** for a month around Christmas. Outside, on Piazza della Scala between the palazzo and the Teatro alla Scala,

GOOD **EATS**

■ **CORSIA DEL GIARDINO**
Enjoy a sweet or savory breakfast or snack in this bistro and bakery's designer setting. They are known for their Sunday brunch, served from 11:30 a.m. to 3:30 p.m. **Via Manzoni 16, tel 02 76280726, €€€**

■ **IL MARCHESINO**
Don't miss the saffron risotto, breaded veal cutlet, or osso buco alla Milanese at La Scala's restaurant, run by the starred chef Gualtiero Marchesi. **Piazza della Scala 2, tel 02 72094338, closed Sat. lunch & Sun., €€€€€**

■ **TRUSSARDI ALLA SCALA**
The view and the kitchen compete with each other in this gourmet restaurant inside the Palazzo Marino alla Scala, headquarters of the house of Trussardi. Luigi Taglienti, a young but highly experienced chef, reinterprets traditional cuisine to make it contemporary. **Piazza della Scala 5, tel 02 80688201, closed Sat. lunch & Sun., €€€€€**

look for a statue of Leonardo surrounded by four of his art students. Its nickname, **"un liter in quater,"** refers to the belief that Leonardo's talent was equal to that of four people put together.

Piazza della Scala 2 • tel 02 88450000 • Metro: Duomo, Line 1, 3

Natural light graces the marble entrance hall of the Gallerie d'Italia in Piazza della Scala.

Gallerie d'Italia

Since 2011, these three historic buildings in the heart of Milan have opened their doors to share the fine art collections owned by the Intesa San Paolo Bank with the public. Art of the 19th century, **"From Canova to Boccioni,"** is exhibited in the beautiful rooms of the Anguissola Antona Traversi and Brentani palaces. A display of **"Works of the 20th Century,"** consisting of 153 works by Italian artists, is on view inside the headquarters of the Banca Commerciale Italiana in Piazza della Scala. It was converted into an exhibition space by Michele De Lucchi to showcase collections from World War II to the present day.

Piazza della Scala 2 • tel 800 167619 • gallerieditalia.com • Closed Mon. • Metro: Duomo, Line 1, 3

Teatro alla Scala

See pp. 62–63.

Via Filodrammatici 2 • tel 02 88791 • teatroallascala.org • Metro: Duomo, Line 1, 3; Montenapoleone, Line 3 • Bus: 61 • Tram: 1, 2

Teatro alla Scala

The Teatro alla Scala is a symbol of Milan, sharing the city's ability to change with the times while keeping its character.

The galleries of the Teatro alla Scala, soaked in centuries of music

Teatro alla Scala opened in 1778 with the first performance of Salieri's opera *Europa riconosciuta (Europe Discovered).* Architect Giuseppe Piermarini was commissioned by Maria Theresa of Austria to build the theater on the site of the church of Santa Maria alla Scala. It originally opened onto a street, not a square, which accounts for its modest facade. Famous composers and conductors including Verdi and Toscanini, directors such as Visconti and Strehler, and dancers such as Rudolf Nureyev, Carla Fracci, and Luciana Savignano have all performed at La Scala.

■ The New Teatro alla Scala

Between 2002 and 2004 La Scala underwent comprehensive renovation to comply with current regulations and to improve its technical facilities. The theater now seats 2,030 people, plus 20 people in the Palco Reale (Royal Box), but the atmosphere remains the same. You can feel the history of the place, where the curtain has opened since 1778, sensing the singers and dancers who gave their best for the long-lost audiences of Austrian Milan, Milan of the Kingdom of Italy, and then of the Italian Republic—and now for you. The drama begins when the lights grow dim, "half lights" when the orchestra starts tuning its instruments, and you feel this could be a night you will remember and be proud to say, "I was there."

■ Opening Night

Should you be so lucky as to be there, opening night at La Scala is filled with drama. Victor De Sabata, artistic director of La Scala from 1929 to 1953, started the tradition of opening the season on **December 7,** the day of St. Ambrose, a patron saint of Milan. The 1951 season opened with *The Sicilian Vespers* in which Maria Callas

made her debut. The opera most frequently performed on opening night is *Don Carlo* by Giuseppe Verdi. This opera has opened the season four times, conducted twice by Claudio Abbado (1968 and 1977) and twice by Riccardo Muti (1992 and 2008). Under age 30? The preview before the opening night is dedicated to you.

■ Museo Teatrale alla Scala

If you have time before the performance (or on another day), wander this fine collection of lavish costumes, set designs, letters, autograph scores, librettos, and ancient musical instruments. True fans may wish to ask to peruse the **Biblioteca Livia Simoni,** an important library of dramatic criticism and theater history.

Largo Ghiringhelli 1 • tel 02 88792473 • teatroallascalla.org • Tickets at central box office in the Duomo Metro station • Same-day standing-room tickets at theater box office 2.5 hours before performance

LA SCALA & AROUND

Futurism & 20th-Century Art

Twentieth-century artistic movements found fertile soil in Milan. Futurism began here, as did the Italian neoclassical movement of the Novecento. Closer to expressionism were the artists of the Movimento di Corrente, active between 1938 and 1943. After World War II Lucio Fontana and Piero Manzoni, the most revolutionary artists of the 20th century, started their artistic careers here.

"Unique Forms of Continuity in Space" by Boccioni (above) is pictured on the back of the Italian 20-cent euro coin. Opposite: Leaders of the Futurist movement. From the left, Aldo Palazzeschi, Carlo Carrà, Giovanni Papini, Umberto Boccioni, and Filippo Tommaso Marinetti.

Home of Futurism

Launched in Milan by Filippo Tommaso Marinetti at the beginning of the 20th century, the artistic movement that became known as Futurism included not only paintings and sculptures, but also poetry, music, architecture, and gastronomy. Rebelling against Romanticism, Futurists embraced modernity and loved cities, speed, noise, and pollution. Their paintings are bold and colorful, and sometimes bewildering—images like towering cities, roaring trains, and war planes whizzing by, depicted in a way to make you feel them with senses beyond sight, so that you smell the gasoline, hear the roar of the engines, and your eyes burn with acrid smoke. Their works sometimes include apologies to violence and progress, with the ultimate aim of celebrating the triumph of man over nature. Not surprisingly, Futuristic ideas were adopted by fascism. For a deeper insight into the atmosphere that encouraged Futurism and the birth of the avant-garde arts of the 20th century, visit **Casa Museo Boschi Di Stefano** (*Via Jan 15,*

tel 02 20240568, fondazioneboschidistefano.it),
Antonio Boschi and Marieda Di Stefano's lifetime
collection donated to the City of Milan for public
viewing. A selection of 2,000 works can be seen
in the 11 rooms (including the bathroom) of
their apartment, with paintings by Mario Sironi,
Morandi, De Pisis, and artists of the Movimento di
Corrente. Also on display are works by De Chirico,
Campigli, Savinio, and Paresce, who were active
in Paris in the 1930s. An entire room is devoted
to Lucio Fontana, another to recent acquisitions,
including works by Piero Manzoni.

MiArt

Spring in Milan is the time for art. Three days in
April belong to MiArt *(miart.it)*, the International
Fair of Modern and Contemporary Art, when
some 150 art galleries display 3,000 works by more
than 500 international artists.

LUCIO **FONTANA**

Lucio Fontana was founder of the
art movement Spatialism, intending
to synthesize color, sound, space,
time, and movement. His work in
Milan is not only in museums:

Via Lanzone 6 Ceramic panels
made by Fontana in the 1950s are
set in the balcony railings.

Duomo Fontana designed the
statue of San Protasio, and his
sketches for the fifth door of the
Duomo are in the Grande Museo
del Duomo (see p. 49).

Via Fosse Ardeatine 4 In the
Carabinieri headquarters is the
remarkable bas-relief "Il Volo
delle Vittorie" ("The Flight of the
Victories"), made in 1939.

Cimitero Monumentale In the
city's cemetery, a polychrome
glazed ceramic angel was
commissioned from Fontana for
the Chinelli family tomb in 1949.

Music

For lovers of music, and not just classical music, Milan hosts a wide variety of events, from jazz to rock, Broadway musicals to classical symphonies. An equally wide variety of venues await, fanning across the city from the notable La Scala.

■ CONSERVATORIO G. VERDI

Ironically, Giuseppe Verdi, who gave his name to this historic institution, was not admitted to the Milan Conservatory because he was considered too old. Today major concert seasons in Milan take place here in the **Sala Verdi.** The renowned conservatory was established in 1807 by royal decree, in a former convent not far from San Babila.

Via Conservatorio 12 • consmilano.it • Metro: San Babila, Line 1 • Bus: 54, 61

■ BLUE NOTE

The first European branch of the famed Blue Note of New York's Greenwich Village opened in the Isola neighborhood in 2003 with a performance by Chick Corea. It continues to be the best Italian venue for jazz, with two shows six nights a week, dinner before the performances, and a **Sunday brunch concert** that includes entertainment for children (2–12 years).

Via Borsieri 37 • tel 02 69016888 • bluenotemilano .com • Closed Mon. • Metro: Garibaldi, Line 2; Isola, Line 5 • Bus: 60 • Tram: 7, 31, 33

■ AUDITORIUM DI MILANO LA VERDI

Located south of the city center, this home of Milan's celebrated orchestra and chorus offers an eclectic program of classical music, ranging from baroque to chamber music, and symphonic to music of lesser known regions.

Via Largo Gustav Mahler • tel 02 83389401 • laverdi.org • Bus: 71 • Tram: 3

■ TEATRO DELLA LUNA

Situated well beyond the city center, this enormous, high-tech venue was created with musical theater in mind. It has room for 1,730 spectators in a large auditorium offering sloped seating. The huge stage, with a record 8,600 square feet (800 sq m), welcomes top Italian and foreign singers and dancers as well as a variety of shows, from popular family-friendly musicals to headliner rock concerts.

Via G. di Vittorio 6, Assago • tel 02 488577516 • teatrodellaluna.com • Metro: Assago Milanofiori Forum, Line 2

The band Boom da Bash performing live before an enthusiastic audience at the MI AMI summer music festival

LA SCALA & AROUND

◼ TEATRO DEGLI ARCIMBOLDI

This huge, impressive modern theater uses sleek architecture to bring lots of light and incredible acoustics. It was designed by Vittorio Gregotti as the flagship of his Grande Bicocca project, redeveloping the former industrial area of Bicocca. The theater plays an important part in Milan's musical scene, showcasing various genres: dance, rock and pop, musicals, and cabaret in a particularly eclectic program.

Viale dell'Innovazione 20 • tel 02 641142200 • teatroarcimboldi.it • Bus: 52, 87 • Tram: 7

SAVVY **TRAVELER**

Milan is flush with musical festivals and events such as the terrific **Cortili Aperti,** when recitals are held in courtyards of private residences, and the extraordinary **Piano City,** when more than 300 piano concerts are performed across the city for three days in May. The first weekend in June brings the festival **MI AMI** (Music Important in Milan), organized by Rockit .it and held on three stages in a park. And don't forget to walk by the **Basilica di San Marco** (see pp. 100–101); all year long, the billboard outside alerts you to concerts performed within.

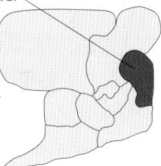

Around the Giardini Pubblici

Few neighborhoods reflect so many different faces of Milanese society as the one that developed around the large green rectangle of the Giardini Pubblici (Public Gardens). Here you will find the homes of the aristocracy designed in the 17th century by architects such as Piermarini, as well as Milan's first public park, influenced by the fashion for Viennese gardens. Wander around the palaces where history was made, at Villa Reale and at Palazzo Serbelloni. Art lovers will find magnificent paintings by Tiepolo at Palazzo Isimbardi, and the Galleria d'Arte Moderna includes Italian masterpieces of the 19th century. Witness how the prosperous bourgeoisie of Milan lived in the Villa Necchi Campiglio, impressive in itself and for its remarkable contents. And beyond Via Vittorio Veneto awaits a worldly neighborhood of shops and restaurants waiting to be discovered.

◖ Villa Belgiojoso
Bonaparte, later the
Villa Reale, now home
of the Galleria d'Arte
Moderna

Around the Giardini Pubblici

Discover the past looking at the palaces of the aristocracy close by the grand public gardens.

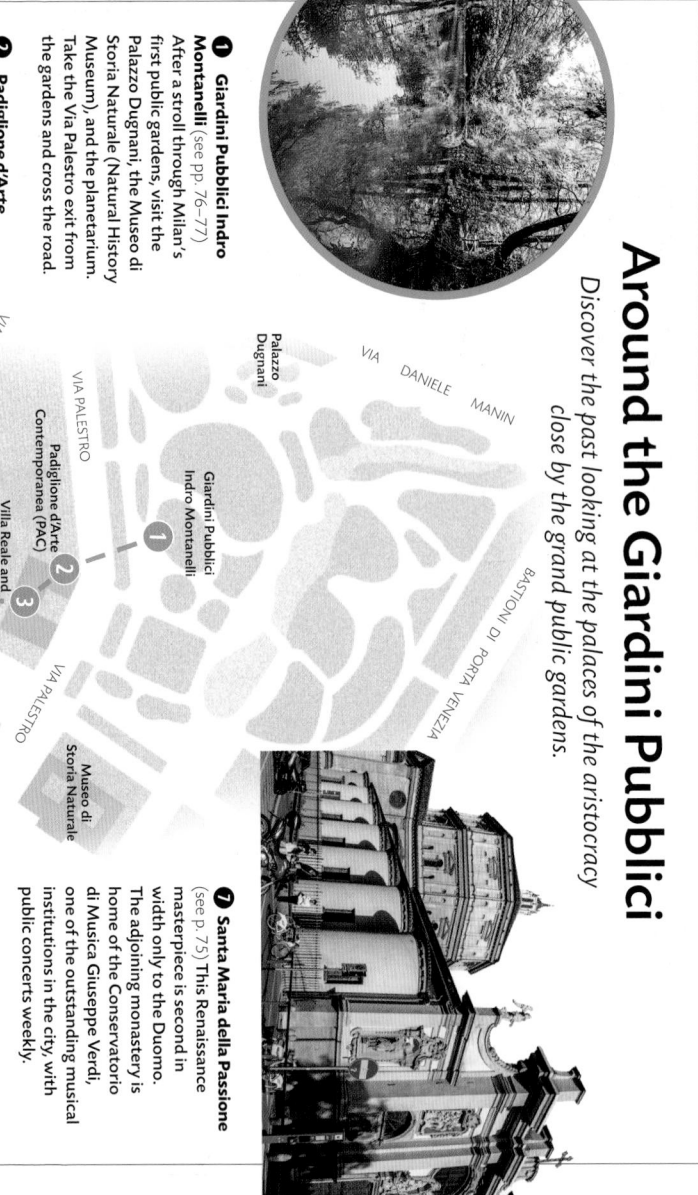

❶ Giardini Pubblici Indro Montanelli (see pp. 76–77)
After a stroll through Milan's first public gardens, visit the Palazzo Dugnani, the Museo di Storia Naturale (Natural History Museum), and the planetarium. Take the Via Palestro exit from the gardens and cross the road.

❷ Padiglione d'Arte Contemporanea (PAC) (see p. 72) Tour one of Italy's earliest exhibition spaces for contemporary art, then head

Palazzo Dugnani

VIA DANIELE MANIN

BASTIONI DI PORTA VENEZIA

Giardini Pubblici Indro Montanelli

VIA DEL VECCHIO POLITECNICO

VIA PALESTRO

PIAZZALE MORANDI

Padiglione d'Arte Contemporanea (PAC)

Villa Reale and Galleria d'Arte Moderna

VIA PALESTRO

Museo di Storia Naturale

VIA MARINA

Palazzo Castiglioni

Palazzo Saporiti

❼ Santa Maria della Passione (see p. 75) This Renaissance masterpiece is second in width only to the Duomo. The adjoining monastery is home of the Conservatorio di Musica Giuseppe Verdi, one of the outstanding musical institutions in the city, with public concerts weekly.

3 Villa Reale / Galleria d'Arte Moderna (see pp. 72–73) Take the time to explore this magical corner, with its neoclassical villa, English garden, and fine collection of modern art. Then go down Via Palestro to Corso Venezia, turn right, and walk to Palazzo Serbelloni at Via Senato.

4 Palazzo Serbelloni (see p. 73) Admire the facade of this neoclassical palace. The magnificent great hall and Piano Napoleonico inside are open to the public on special occasions. Turn left on Via Senato, then left again on Via Mozart to Villa Necchi Campiglio.

5 Villa Necchi Campiglio (see p. 74) The stylish appeal of this intact house-museum designed by Portaluppi is that it is like entering a huge film set for a movie of the 1930s. Continue along Via Mozart, turn right on Via Vivaio, then right again on Corso Monforte.

6 Palazzo Isimbardi (see pp. 74–75) This is a particularly interesting place for architecture lovers. From Corso Monforte you can admire its ancient entrance, only rarely open; inside is a magnificent 16th-century ceremonial courtyard. The wing designed by Muzio in the 1940s faces Via Vivaio. Follow Via Conservatorio all the way until you reach the *conservatorio* and Santa Maria della Passione.

Via Marina

VIA DEI BOSCHETTI

Palazzo del Senato (Archivio di Stato)

VIA SAN PRIMO

VIA GABRIO SERBELLONI

CORSO VENEZIA

VIA DELLA SPIGA

VIA VERRI

Ex Seminario

SENATO

VIA

CORSO VENEZIA

VIA SAN DAMIANO

Palazzo Serbelloni ④

VIA MOZART

⑤ Villa Necchi Campiglio

Istituto dei Ciechi

VIA VIVAIO

Palazzo Isimbardi ⑥

CORSO MONFORTE

VIA PIETRO

VIA CONSERVATORIO

MASCAGNI

VIA LIVORNO

VINCENZO BELLINI

VIA VIVAIO

Santa Maria della Passione

⑦ Conservatorio di Musica Giuseppe Verdi

0   200 meters
0   200 yards

AROUND THE GIARDINI PUBBLICI

AROUND THE GIARDINI PUBBLICI   DISTANCE: 1.2 MILES (2 KM)
TIME: ABOUT 6 HOURS   METRO START: PALESTRO, LINE 1

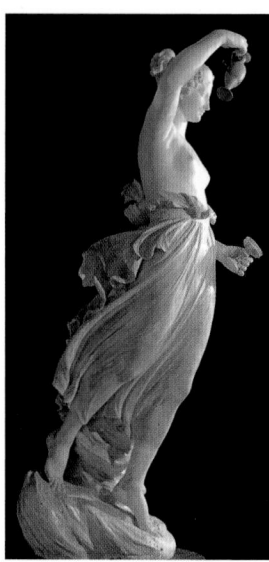

Graceful "Hebe" by Canova, one of the masterpieces waiting at the Gallery of Modern Art

Giardini Pubblici Indro Montanelli

1 See pp. 76–77.

Bet. Porta Venezia, Via Manin, Via Palestro, and Corso Venezia • Museo di Storia Naturale: Corso Venezia 55 • tel 02 88463337• Closed Mon. • € • Planetario Ulrico Hoepli: tel 02 88463340 • Metro: Palestro, Line 1; Turati, Line 3 • Bus: 61, 94 • Tram: 1, 9

Padiglione d'Arte Contemporanea (PAC)

2 Following the heavy bombing of 1943 that destroyed, along with much of the city, the stables of the Villa Reale on this site, the City of Milan commissioned architect Ignazio Gardella to design the Pavilion of Contemporary Art for the **Civiche raccolte del XX secolo** (20th-Century Civic Collections), a "second chapter" devoted to the contemporary art of the nearby Galleria d'Arte Moderna. Opened in 1954, this architectural space was planned so that walls and panels can be moved to change the size, lighting, and flow of an exhibit, making it popular among artists and spectators alike. Since the 1970s it has exclusively held temporary exhibitions of contemporary art. Although destroyed by a Mafia bomb in 1993, it was rebuilt to the original plan in 1996.

Via Palestro 14 • tel 02 88446359 • pacmilano.it • Closed Mon. • €€ • Metro: Palestro, Line 1 • Bus: 61, 92

Villa Reale/Galleria d'Arte Moderna

3 History and art are often intertwined at Villa Reale, one of the major neoclassical buildings in the city constructed for his own use by the diplomat Ludovico Barbiano di Belgiojoso in what was, at the time, an area outside the city. The task was given to Piermarini, the architect of La Scala and Palazzo Reale, who subcontracted the work to Leopoldo Pollack. The building has two fronts, one on the current Via Palestro and the other, main one facing the beautiful gardens designed by Count Ercole Silva, the first example of the English garden style in Milan. Adults may only enter this charming little park if accompanied by a child.

Since 1921 several of the city's art collections have been exhibited on three floors of the romantic villa, which became "Reale" in the Napoleonic period. The tour starts with neoclassical masterpieces by Appiani, Canova, and others, followed by works of Lombard Romanticism, the Scapigliatura school, and the divisionist period. On the ground floor, the **Vismara Collection** is devoted to French and Italian painting and sculpture of the 20th century. Up on the second floor, the **Grassi Collection** features works of the 19th and 20th centuries. The rooms themselves are equally interesting, with frescoes and furniture of the neoclassical period.

Via Palestro 16 • tel 02 88445947 • Closed Mon. • € • Metro: Palestro, Line 1 • Bus: 61, 92

Palazzo Serbelloni

4 Piermarini's eternal rival Simone Cantoni designed the monumental architecture of the Palazzo Serbelloni, built in the neoclassical style in the late 18th century. Its impressive facade includes elements of a Greek temple, with a balcony above, clean and austere in contrast to the opulence glimpsed inside, such as the entrance hall awash with trompe l'oeil frescoes. One of the first great residences built outside the circle of the Navigli canals, it was the home of many famous people, including Napoleon and Josephine Bonaparte. They stayed here for three months, preferring it to Villa Reale. You can visit for free—but by reservation only, so plan ahead—to gape at the grand Napoleonic hall, restored to the original decadent stucco, marble columns, and chandeliers after being damaged by the bombings of World War II.

Corso Venezia 16 • tel 02 76007687 • fondazioneserbelloni.com • Guided tours by reservation only • Metro: Palestro, Line 1

Villa Necchi Campiglio

5 This house-museum is one of the real off-the-beaten-track gems of Milan, complete with beautiful gardens graced by a decorative pool and giant magnolia trees. It opened to the public in 2008 after a long process of restoration directed by architect Piero Castellini. Today it provides visitors a unique insight into the daily life of a privileged family of Milan in the 1930s, from the reception hall to the bathrooms. Home to the Necchi Campiglio family, wealthy Lombard manufacturers, it was equipped with the most modern technical devices of the day, including an elevator, a dumbwaiter, and a heated swimming pool. In recent years, the house, owned by FAI (Fondo Ambiente Italiano), has received two valuable collections: the **Claudia Gian Ferrari Collection** of early 20th-century works of art by Arturo Martini, Georgio Morandi, and others; and the **collection of 18th-century paintings and decorative arts** donated by Alighiero and Emilietta de' Micheli, including paintings by Canaletto, Tiepolo, Marieschi, and Venetian rococo artist Rosalba Carriera, as well as fine porcelain.

Via Mozart 14 • tel 02 76340121 • fondoambiente.it • Closed Mon.–Tues. • Guided tours only • €€€ • Metro: Palestro, Line 1 • Bus: 54, 61, 94

Wooden globe dating from 1688 made by Giovanni Jacopo de' Rossi, in the Palazzo Isimbardi

Palazzo Isimbardi

6 Headquarters of the province of Milan in 1935, the 15th-century Palazzo Isimbardi, with its extension in functionalist style designed by Giovanni Muzio in 1940, is one of the least known and most interesting places in the city. Visits are very limited (usually the first Friday and third Wednesday of the month), but its artistic heritage is particularly rich, starting with Tiepolo's work depicting the **"Ascent of Angelo della Vecchia in the Name of Virtue"** in the Sala della Giunta, and the painting **"Episode of the Visconti"** by Francesco Hayez. There are also many fine 19th-century works by Leonardo Bazzaro and Luigi Conconi from Lombardy, Lorenzo

Delleani from Piedmont, and Edoardo Dalbon from Naples. Also worth seeing is the **courtyard** that lies behind the building's 19th-century facade. It is the old courtyard of the palazzo of the counts of Taverna, with 16th-century terra-cotta paving embellished with marble from Candoglia, the same as that used for the construction of the Duomo.

Corso Monforte 35 • tel 02 77404343 • provincia.milano.it • Free guided tours, reservations required • Metro: San Babila, Palestro, Line 1 • Bus: 54, 61, 94 • Tram: 9, 23, 29, 30

Santa Maria della Passione

7 Among the jewels behind the baroque facade of this basilica are "**The Deposition,**" attributed to Luini, in the right transept; the altarpiece with the "**Last Supper**" by Gaudenzio Ferrari; and the intense "**San Carlo Fasting**" by Daniele Crespi in the first chapel. Recognized as one of the masterpieces of the Renaissance, the church itself is second in width only to the Duomo. The **Sala Capitolare** (Chapter House) is decorated with frescoes by Bergognone depicting elders of the church, patron saints of the order, and canonical Lateran saints. Also worthy of note are the two **wooden organs** of the church: The one on the right side is by Antegnati, while the one on the left is by the organ builder Valvassori (who made the organ of the Duomo). The musical vocation of Santa Maria della Passione finds its fulfillment in the ancient monastery adjacent to the church, home of the historic Milan Conservatory (see p. 66), the city's most important music academy. Here a functioning concert hall hosts musicians and orchestras from around the world. Concerts are typically held on Wednesday and/or Thursday nights.

Via Conservatorio 12 • tel 02 76021370 • Metro: San Babila, Line 1 • Bus: 54, 61

(see p. 66)

GOOD **EATS**

■ CAFFETTERIA OF VILLA NECCHI CAMPIGLIO
Designed as a winter garden between the pool and the tennis court of the museum, this café is a lovely place for a quick stop, especially on a sunny day when you can sit outside.
Via Mozart 10, tel 02 76020873, €€€

■ JOIA KITCHEN BISTRO
From Monday to Friday the room opposite the kitchen of the Joia restaurant, the first vegetarian restaurant in Europe to be awarded a Michelin star, is transformed into a bistro where you can still taste innovative dishes but at lower prices.
Via Panfilo Castaldi 18, tel 02 2952 2124, closed Sat.–Sun., €€€

■ SWISS CORNER LOUNGE BISTRO
The ground floor of the Swiss skyscraper is a place with two souls: one devoted to exhibitions and the other to dining and entertainment, with the chance to enjoy Swiss delicacies from 10 a.m. to 2 a.m. The restaurant is very popular at *aperitivo* time.
Piazza Cavour & Via Palestro, tel 02 76390698, €€€

Giardini Pubblici Indro Montanelli

Milan's beloved public gardens highlight nature's beauty through graceful plantings and intriguing museums.

Skeleton of a sperm whale, one of the many fascinating exhibits in the Museo di Storia Naturale

The Giardini, as the Giardini Pubblici are known, welcome visitors in every season: for brisk winter walks along frost-covered meadows, springtime strolls under blooming plum and cherry trees, summertime picnics on shady lawns, and perhaps most spectacular of all, autumn visits, when bright yellow ginkgo leaves carpet the paths. After wandering outdoors, head inside to see whale skeletons, dinosaur reconstructions, and more at the natural history museum, or look to the stars at the Planetario, with shows on weekend afternoons.

■ Palazzo Dugnani

Lovely Giardini Pubblici was once the private park of Palazzo Dugnani, built in the 17th century and later restored in the rococo style. Home to many Milanese noble families, the building's ownership transferred to the city in 1846 and it subsequently served as a museum, a high school, and a site of civil marriages (in its beautiful ballroom). The large reception room, two stories high, is notable for its frescoes created in 1731 by Giambattista Tiepolo. The palazzo is currently closed for renovation.

■ Museo di Storia Naturale

Milan's Museum of Natural History moved from Palazzo Dugnani to this part of the gardens and this unusual Romanesque, Gothic Byzantine–style building. Inspired by the great natural history museums of other countries, particularly the one in London, the collection remains one of the most important in the world, despite damage by bombing in World War II. Of particular note are its many dioramas of arctic, jungle, and prairie landscapes stuffed with taxidermy. Look, too, for the life-size triceratops.

■ Planetario Ulrico Hoepli

The Civic Planetarium was inaugurated in 1930, having been presented to the city by the publisher Ulrico Hoepli. The building was designed in the neoclassical style by Piero Portaluppi "in a place that was within the body of the metropolis and at the same time secluded," that is, within the Giardini Pubblici, toward Corso Venezia. It is still Italy's largest planetarium, with a dome 66 feet (20 m) in diameter and an octagonal room with the capacity to host more than 300 people at each show. A guided projection tour of the night sky (in Italian) fascinates visitors every Saturday and Sunday afternoon; children in particular will enjoy swiveling in their seats as they track the sky above.

Museo di Storia Naturale: Corso Venezia 55 • tel 02 88463337 • Closed Mon. • Metro: Palestro, Line 1 • Tram: 9 • Planetario Ulrico Hoepli: Corso Venezia 57 • tel 02 88463340 • Opening times vary • Metro: Palestro, Line 1; Turati, Line 3 • Bus: 61, 94 • Tram: 1, 9

Art Nouveau

In the late 19th century, the art nouveau movement swept through architecture and the decorative arts in Europe and beyond. Avowedly modern, it sought to transform design across many disciplines and champion craft over the mass-produced, drawing inspiration from natural and geometric forms to produce elegant and often distinctly colored and decorated artifacts and buildings. This was especially popular in Italy, where it was known as the "Liberty" style.

Two striking facades tell the story of Italy's Liberty style: Colored majolica embellishes Casa Galimberti (above), while a vintage photograph (opposite) shows the strength of the aquaculture pavilion at Expo 1906.

New City, New Style

Milan was ripe for art nouveau at the time of the movement's ascendancy, thanks to the growth of the city, which meant new buildings, and the rise of a prosperous middle and industrialist class for whom modernity and culture—art and architecture in particular—became increasingly important. In 1906 Milan hosted an international "Expo," for which some 225 new buildings were created, many of them in the new style. As a result, the city has hundreds of surviving Liberty buildings, many retaining the new or reworked materials of art nouveau—iron, glass, and concrete—in both striking facades and beautiful decorative details.

Stylish Scandal

Milan's greatest exponent of the new style was Giuseppe Sommaruga (1867–1917). His first major work was the **Palazzo Castiglioni** (*Corso Venezia 47–49*), built between 1901 and 1904 and seen as a blueprint for art nouveau across Italy. The Milanese called it the Ca' de Ciapp, or House of Buttocks, after two provocative nude statues on the entrance gate that had to be removed within 15 days of their unveiling.

Ceramic and Concrete

Another major player was Giovanni Battista Bossi (1864–1924). He moved from Sommaruga's use of statues as a decorative motif to beautifully colored majolica, seen to dazzling effect on **Casa Galimberti** *(Via Malpighi 3)*, where male and female figures are intertwined with a wealth of foliage and flowers. A few doors away, the same architect showed versatility with **Casa Guazzoni** *(Via Malpighi 12)*; here majolica is replaced by a profusion of decoration in iron and concrete. You will stumble across these and other Liberty buildings as you explore Milan, as well as art nouveau furniture, jewelry, and other artifacts. Ask at visitor centers about special guided walks.

ART NOUVEAU GEMS

Acquario Civico *(Viale Gadio 2)*
The lone survivor of the Expo 1906 Parco Sempione buildings

Casa Berri Meregalli *(Via Cappuccini 8)* Note the figures that adorn the front of this private home

Casa Campanini *(Via Bellini 11)* This remarkable facade boasts exceptional wrought-iron balconies.

Cinema Dumont *(Via Frisi 2)* Now a library, but with a notable surviving facade and hall

Palazzina Liberty *(Largo Marinai d'Italia)* Formerly the Verziere fruit and vegetable market

Via Pisacane The many Liberty buildings on this street form an art nouveau open-air museum.

Viale Piave 42 The former Kursaal Diana is now the Sheraton Diana Majestic hotel.

AROUND THE GIARDINI PUBBLICI

Aperitivi

It's six o'clock in the evening, time for *aperitivi*, a typical Milanese tradition of a predinner drink as a transition from the stress of the day to the delights of the evening. Some places offer chips, olives, or dainty snacks, but most Milanese bars opt for "happy hour," huge buffets that can more than replace dinner.

■ FASHION AND THE GREAT CLASSICS
You will find the Milanese tradition of aperitivo going strong throughout the city, from tried-and-true to up-and-coming spots frequented by those in the know. For a drink to start the evening near the Giardini Pubblici, head to the **Sheraton Diana Majestic** (*Viale Piave 42*) and join in with the cool crowd at **h club > diana,** the hottest spot in town. Trendy music, cocktails, and a luxurious garden set the tone for this thoroughly enjoyable social scene. A fashionable alternative in the Sempione district is **55 Milano** (*Via Piero della Francesca 55, formerly Roialto*). Within its vast space, this bar welcomes you to a happy hour unique in the city: Ten food stations serve all kinds of tempting delicacies and drink from 6 p.m. to 11 p.m. If you're in the fun Isola district, you can enjoy the decidedly more alternative, creative atmosphere of **Frida** (*Via Pollaiuolo 3*),
a colorful bar with an eco-fashion shop attached. In the Porta Garibaldi area, join architects and designers at their favorite meeting place, **Radetzky Café** (*Corso Garibaldi 105*). Or you can visit the past at two historic destinations: **Bar Magenta** (*Via Carducci 13*), with remarkable art nouveau decoration dating from 1907, and **Belle Aurore** (*Via Abamonti 1*), imbued with a Paris bistro atmosphere that has remained unchanged over many years.

■ FIRST-RATE COCKTAILS
If you're seeking a cocktail mixed to order back near the public gardens, head to **Bar Basso** (*Via Plinio 39*). An American cocktail bar par excellence, it is famous for inventing the Negroni Sbagliato, a variation on the classic Milanese drink. Alternatively, the tiny and creative **Nottingham Forest** (*Viale Piave 1*) will amaze you with excellent molecular cocktails.

With a vintage atmosphere and a long tradition, Bar Basso is still the point of reference for classic cocktails, with a list of about 500 different options.

■ BEERS AND PUBS

Have a drink the English way at the **Old Fox Pub** (*Piazza Sant'Agostino*), in the Ticinese and Navigli area, where you can enjoy a wide choice of draft beers, lagers, ales, and bitter ales as well as interesting bottled beers, all accompanied by hot and cold snacks.

Craft beer enthusiasts and sports fans meet up at **Scott Duff Club** (*Via Volta 13*) in the heart of Milan's lively Brera and Garibaldi nightlife district. In addition to an interesting selection of draft and bottled beers from all over Europe, the club's five large screens keep sport addicts happy. For excellent local cask beer, including a selection fresh from the city's Birrificio Lambrate, make your way to Southeast Milan and the unpretentious **Hop** (*Viale Regina Margherita 16*), where you will find others who share your passion. Weather permitting, you can sit outdoors.

IN **THE KNOW**

Many different explanations have been offered for the ritual of *aperitivo (apéritif* for the French), but most agree its primary reason is to stimulate the appetite. Gin, vermouth, and Campari together form the classic Italian aperitivo, the Negroni.

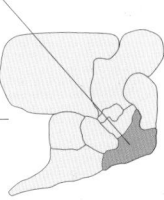

Southeast Milan

The southeast area of Milan is full of history. Here every monument can claim to have not just one, but at least three lives. Within the ancient Spanish walls, buildings have changed purpose as events warranted. For example, the Rotonda della Besana was originally a cemetery for the poor, then a center for the chronically ill, and today it is the kingdom of young children as MUBA, the Museo dei Bambini (Children's Museum). Its garden and the Giardino della Guastalla are little green jewels in this developed area. Also worth a wander are the beautifully proportioned courtyards of Ca' Granda, where you'll mingle with university students. This part of Milan hosts several distinctive places of worship, including the city's great synagogue, reconstructed along with many other buildings after the bombings of World War II, and the art-filled Basilica di Sant'Eufemia. Perhaps most memorable will be your visit to the odd church of San Bernardino alle Ossa, with a chapel covered in the bones of Milanese recovered from city cemeteries closed in the 1600s, many victims of the plague.

◯ **La Rotonda della Besana, with the church of San Michele at its the center, is now home to MUBA, the Museo dei Bambini.**

Southeast Milan

In this changing part of Milan, a cemetery has become a museum and a hospital is now a university, but the places of worship remain.

3 Synagogue of Via Guastalla (see p. 87) **Opened in 1892 and designed by Beltrami, Milan's Great Synagogue has the typical basilica plan of a nave with two side aisles. Cross the road to the garden.**

4 Giardino della Guastalla (see p. 87) **This city garden was once home to a college for educating "impoverished girls of aristocratic families." Exit the garden on Via Francesco Sforza, turn left on Via Laghetto, and cross Piazza Santo Stefano until you get to Via Verziere.**

5 San Bernardino alle Ossa (see p. 88) **Pay a tremulous visit to the somewhat creepy ossuary chapel of San Bernardino, then walk back through Piazza Santo Stefano, follow Via Festa del Perdono (right next to Via Laghetto) to the end, at the university.**

❷ Palazzo di Giustizia (see p. 86) Clad in white marble and housing the Court of Milan, this is one of the city's best examples of fascist architecture. Walk around to Via Freguglia, following it down to the corner between Via San Barnaba and Via Guastalla.

CORSO DI PORTA VITTORIA

VIA FREGUGLIA

❷ Palazzo di Giustizia

VIA MANARA

VIA ENRICO BESANA

Rotonda della Besana ❶

❸ Synagogue of Via Guastalla

SAN BARNABA

Santa Maria della Pace

Santi Paolo e Barnaba

VIA DAVERIO

Ospedale Maggiore

VIALE REGINA MARGHERITA

❶ Rotonda della Besana (see p. 86) Visit MUBA, the new Museo dei Bambini, and its garden surrounded by a beautiful circular colonnade. Walk to Via San Barnaba, then right on Via Manara.

❼ Basilica dei Santi Apostoli and Nazaro Maggiore (see pp. 88–89) This is one of the four Ambrosian basilicas built by the bishop in Milan in the fourth century. From here, follow Via Osti, crossing Corso di Porta Romana to Via Lentasio. Then continue straight to Piazza Sant'Eufemia.

❽ Basilica di Sant'Eufemia (see p. 89) Visit for the amazing works of art within, including "Pentecost" by Peterzano. Next turn left onto Corso Italia and continue straight.

❻ Ca' Granda (see pp. 90–91) In the mid-1400s this was the most modern hospital in Europe. Now it is occupied by the Università degli Studi. From here, walk next door to the basilica.

❾ Santa Maria dei Miracoli presso San Celso (see p. 89) Traditionally, newly married couples come for a blessing to this late 15th-century church. The streets nearby are filled with bars and restaurants to end your day.

SOUTHEAST MILAN DISTANCE: 1.7 MILES (2.8 KM) TIME: ABOUT 5 HOURS METRO START: PORTA ROMANA, LINE 3

The church of San Michele, now home to a children's museum

Rotonda della Besana

1 The Rotonda della Besana is worth a visit for its quirky architecture, tranquil atmosphere, and interesting history. A morning stroll around its rounded baroque forms is a nice way to start off the day. Wander through the porches of the interior colonnade surrounding the large lawn, at the center of which stands the church of **San Michele ai Nuovi Sepolcri,** laid out in the form of a Greek cross. If you have children with you, this is a must-stop: In 2014 the deconsecrated building became headquarters of **MUBA, the Museo dei Bambini di Milano** (Children's Museum of Milan; see p. 30). This is a happy ending for the Besana: Originally built as a cemetery for the Ospedale Maggiore (Greater Hospital) to bury the dead outside its walls, there were plans to make it the Pantheon of the Kingdom of Italy, but this faded with the fall of Napoleon. Under the Austrians it became a military warehouse and stables, then a shelter for the chronically ill, and then a laundry. Photographers take note: The compound's unusual perspectives make for intriguing images.

Via Besana 12 • tel 02 43980402 • muba.it • Bus: 73, 77, 84 • Tram: 9, 12, 23, 27

Palazzo di Giustizia

2 Milan's courthouse was built between 1932 and 1940 following the monumental-rationalist style of architecture prevalent during fascist times. Its facade, covered in gleaming white marble, is decorated with Latin quotes about justice. Inside, the building has mosaics and bas-reliefs illustrating the history of justice in Roman times. Officially, you cannot visit unless you have some business to conduct inside the courthouse, but as it's the seat for several public offices, no one will stop you from going in and looking around.

Corso di Porta Vittoria • Tram: 12, 23, 27

Synagogue of Via Guastalla

3 Since its construction in 1892, the Great Synagogue of Via Guastalla has been the center for the Jewish community of Milan, now numbering some 7,000 people. The original synagogue was built by Luca Beltrami, one of the most important and active Milanese architects bridging the 19th and 20th centuries. All that remains is the facade decorated with mosaics of cobalt blue and gold: The building was destroyed by bombing in World War II and had to be completely reconstructed. In 1997, the synagogue was again rebuilt with the addition of 23 stained-glass windows by the American artist Roger Selden. Interesting guided tours are held on the European Day of Jewish Culture (early September) and other times; reservations are required.

Via Guastalla 19 • tel 02 5512029 • Email: desk@rabbinato-milano.it • Bus: 60, 77, 94 • Tram: 12

Giardino della Guastalla

4 Much enjoyed by the young people attending the nearby Università Statale, the Giardino della Guastalla takes its name from Paola Ludovica Torelli, Countess of Guastalla. In the 16th century, she acquired land at Porta Tosa (Porta Vittoria) and created this popular garden with some fine architectural features. Enjoy meandering the pathways of this small city park; although today there is no lake, you will find a baroque fish pond of almost 5,400 square feet (502 sq m), with two terraces and four flights of steps to get your exercise. Tucked among the ancient trees is a 17th-century grotto where you can view a group of statues in terra-cotta and plaster depicting Mary Magdalene with the angels. Look, too, for the neoclassical temple designed by Luigi Cagnola.

Entrances from Via Francesco Sforza, Via San Barnaba, and Via Guastalla • Bus: 60, 77, 94 • Tram: 12

SOUTHEAST MILAN

IN **THE KNOW**

Behind the octagonal lantern of San Bernardino alle Ossa is a monument to Carlo Porta. This used to be the area of Verziere, the fruit-and-vegetable market, where the greatest poet in the Milanese dialect drew inspiration for his works.

San Bernardino alle Ossa

5 Between Verziere, the old fruit-and-vegetable market, and Piazza Santo Stefano—dominated by the late 16th-century facade of the **Basilica of Santo Stefano Maggiore**—stands one of the places that is both evocative of Milan and somewhat disturbing: the church of San Bernardino alle Ossa. Inside, to the right of the entrance, is the famous and bizarre ossuary chapel, completely covered with skulls and human bones set in various symbols and patterns. The result is an example of macabre rococo, dominated by a glowing fresco in the domed ceiling, the work of Venetian Sebastiano Ricci.

Via Merlo 4 • Metro: Duomo, Line 1, 3

Ca' Granda

6 See pp. 90–91.

Via Festa del Perdono 7 • tel 02 503111 • Crypt of the Chiesa dell'Annunciata closed Fri.–Sun. • Metro: Missori, Line 3 • Bus: 54, 60, 65 • Tram: 12, 23, 24, 27

Basilica dei Santi Apostoli and Nazaro Maggiore

7 As part of his evangelizing tour between 382 and 386, St. Ambrose founded this church to house the relics of the apostles Andrew, John, and Thomas. Their remains, along with those of local martyr St. Nazarius, are still present under the two altars in the choir. Although the basilica has been damaged and restored several times over the centuries, you can still see traces of the original early Christian masonry on the walls. Also notable are the transept paintings: "Last Supper" by Bernardino Lanino and "Passion of Jesus" by Luini. During the

The geometrical perfection of Ca' Granda, the hospital designed by Filarete

Renaissance the **Trivulzio Chapel,** designed by Bramantino, was added to the basilica; look to the second tier for the family sarcophagi.

Piazza San Nazaro in Brolo 5 • Metro: Missori, Line 3

Basilica di Sant'Eufemia

8 The church of St. Eufemia, overlooking one of the prettiest squares of Milan, was founded in the fifth century. What is seen today is the result of numerous rebuilding operations, the last in 1870 when Enrico Terzaghi redesigned the facade and interior in the neo-Gothic style. Look inside for the painting "Pentecost" by Simone Peterzano, the artist who taught Caravaggio. It was moved here from the nearby **church of San Paolo Converso,** now deconsecrated.

Piazza Sant'Eufemia 2 • Metro: Missori, Line 3

Santa Maria dei Miracoli presso San Celso

9 Since the 16th century it has been the tradition for couples who marry in Milan to bring flowers in tribute to the "Madonna degli sposi," a baroque sculpture by Annibale Fontana on the altar of the Madonna in this church. Gian Giacomo Dolcebuono started building here in 1493 on the site of one founded by St. Ambrose, where the remains of Christian martyrs St. Nazarius and St. Celsus had been found. Next to its 17th-century facade is the tiny 11th-century Romanesque **church of San Celso.** Behind the building, at Via Vigoni no. 10, is a lovely little garden named after the popular journalist Enzo Biagi.

Corso Italia 37 • Metro: Missori, Line 3 • Tram: 15

Ca' Granda

This immense centuries-old hospital complex, now part of Milan University, retains much of its beautiful Renaissance architecture.

The Cortile della Farmacia of Ca' Granda with its double colonnade

The Ca' Granda complex is today home to the arts, history, and law faculties of Milan University, but it began life in the 1450s as part of a plan by Francesco Sforza, then the city's ruler, to consolidate Milan's 30 or more small hospitals into one "large house" *(ca' granda)*. Also known as the Ospedale Maggiore, it provided health care to the poor. New building continued as late as the 18th century, and the complex remained a hospital until 1942. Despite serious damage in World War II, much of the Ca' Granda survives or has been restored.

SOUTHEAST MILAN

THE FACADE

The Ca' Granda's striking facade carries the terra-cotta decorations that grace many Milan buildings, but these show elements from the 15th century. You can make out the three main phases of the building's construction, first by a Tuscan architect, Antonio Averlino (known as Filarete), who envisaged the hospital as part of a grander scheme to transform part of Milan into an ideal Renaissance city. The distinctive right wing dates from the 15th century, while the main building, including the main baroque entrance, dates from the 17th century.

CORTILE DI RICHINI

Inside, the complex was divided into several courtyards and separate wards for men and women. Two side courtyards are quartered by paths to form a cross, a deliberate piece of religious significance. Between these courtyards and their four identical smaller courtyards stretches another, larger courtyard, known as the Cortile Maggiore or Cortile di Richini after its architect, Francesco Maria Richini. A glorious medley of arches and arcades, it dates from 1625.

CRYPT OF THE CHIESA DELL'ANNUNCIATA

Before leaving the Ca' Granda be sure to visit the Chiesa dell'Annunciata (Church of the Annunciation), built by Richini in a corner of the *cortile* in 1637. Its artistic highlight is a painting of the "Annunciation" (1639) by the baroque painter Guercino. Downstairs, in the church's crypt, walls show traces of 17th-century frescoes, along with the names of 141 victims who died during "The Five Days of Milan," an uprising against the Austrians in 1848. The rebels were also buried here (but later moved to a new monument), along with an estimated 500,000 other people, mostly hospital patients who died between 1473 and 1695, the year when burials on the site were no longer permitted.

SOUTHEAST MILAN

Via Festa del Perdono 7 • tel 02 503111 • Crypt of the Chiesa dell'Annunciata closed Fri.–Sun. • Metro: Missori, Line 3 • Bus: 54, 60, 65 • Tram: 12, 23, 24, 27

The Circles of Milan

"The plan of the city is round and this wonderful roundness is the mark of its perfection," wrote Bonvesin de la Riva in 1288. The city has grown in circles, and being familiar with them helps in moving around Milan as well as in finding out about its history and urban development. Successive rings enclose the Roman city, the medieval one, the Spanish one, and the one redesigned at the end of the 19th century by Cesare Beruto, who created Milan's first city-development plan.

The two Porta Nuovas: A detail from the arches of the old Porta Nuova (above), and the modern glass curves of Gae Aulenti Plaza in the new development of Porta Nuova (opposite)

La Cerchia dei Navigli

The Circle of Navigli (canals) was built in the 12th century as a defensive structure against Barbarossa, along with six fortified gates. Two of these survive today, the **Porta Nuova** between Via Manzoni and Piazza Cavour, and the single-arched **Porta Ticinese**, flanked by two towers. At the end of the 14th century Gian Galeazzo and Filippo Maria Visconti made the defensive moat navigable to facilitate trade and supplies. The canal was linked to the Naviglio della Martesana in about 1497, and it continued to connect the Ticino and Adda Rivers until the 1930s. This is when the "water city" was covered over and replaced by a network of roads, also known as the Cerchia dei Navigli, that still surrounds the medieval city. **Naviglio Grande** and **Naviglio Pavese** survived, and today are favorite spots for a stroll or sightseeing cruise.

La Cerchia dei Bastioni

Where defensive walls were built on the orders of Spanish governor Ferrante Gonzaga is today another insurmountable yet invisible barrier, one monitored by 43 video cameras surrounding the restricted traffic zone known as Area C. This congestion charge zone, created by the city council in 2012, corresponds to the **Cerchia dei Bastioni,** the route of the Spanish walls built from 1546 to 1560, tripling the size of the city and forming the longest system of walls in Europe, with a length of nearly 7 miles (11 km). You can still see some sections of the wall in Piazza Medaglie d'Oro and in Via Vittorio Veneto.

The Outer Circle

After the Unification of Italy in 1861, Milan expanded and a new outer ring road was created around the city, with wide avenues named after Italian regions, such as Viale Liguria and Viale Molise. This was part of the **Beruto City Plan** of 1849, which lasted until after World War II.

THE **GATES OF MILAN**

Arches of Porta Nuova
At the end of Via Manzoni, this military monument was built as a defensive fortification after the destruction caused by Barbarossa.

Porta Cicca The nickname of Porta Ticinese, built by Cagnola in Napoleonic times

Porta Sempione This 19th-century triumphal arch traces its origins to the Roman walls of Milan.

Porta Ticinese Antica One of the main gates of the medieval walls, formed of a single round arch

Porta Venezia The former Porta Orientale was the first gate in the defensive Spanish walls to be renewed in the 19th century.

Unexpected Milan

In the busy city that is Milan, it is sometimes good to get away from it all.

In a city where fashions are born, it is nonetheless possible to find places and

activities that are off the beaten track. Take a break and picnic in the heart of the

city or enjoy a swim in a thermal bath with echoes of ancient Rome.

■ CASCINA CUCCAGNA

Between Porta Romana and Corso Lodi in southeast Milan, in what was once open countryside, survives this former 17th-century farmhouse—a wonderful oasis in the heart of the city. Now converted into a fashionable bar and restaurant, **Un Posto a Milano,** it features seasonal produce that is locally sourced and traceable. Here, too, is **La Bottega di Campagna Amica,** a shop selling products of the Filiera Agricola Italiana (Italian Agricultural Food Chain).

Via Cuccagna 2/4 • tel 02 83421007 • cuccagna .org • Metro: Porta Romana or Lodi TIBB, Line 3 • Bus: 62, 77, 90, 91, 92 • Tram: 9, 16

■ THERMAL BATHS

History and well-being are combined at **QC Termemilano.** Here the opulence of ancient Rome joins the art nouveau setting of a former horse-drawn tram station and depot, surrounded by the *mura spagnole* (Spanish walls) built by

Ferrante I Gonzaga between 1548 and 1562. Located in the Porta Romana district of southeast Milan, this is the place to enjoy a hot tub hydromassage, steam baths, and other spa treatments.

Cnr. Piazza Medaglie d'Oro 2 & Via Filippetti • tel 02 55199367 • termemilano.com • €€€€€

■ PICNIC IN THE PARK

What could be nicer than a luxurious picnic on a sunny day? If you're in the Ticinese and Navigli area, order the best picnic lunch in the city from the **California Bakery,** a chain with about a dozen stores in Milan. Then head to **Parco delle Basiliche** (see p. 22).

Piazza Sant'Eustorgio 4 • tel 02 39811750 • californiabakery.it • €€€

■ DIALOGUE IN THE DARK

An exhibition without exhibits: Dialogo nel Buio, or Dialogue in the Dark, is an extraordinary experience that since

A whirlpool bath by the so-called *mura spagnole* (Spanish walls) of the 16th century

2002 has been enabling visitors to "see" in a new way, using their senses of touch, hearing, smell, and taste to explore the unseen. Blind guides take groups of eight people through rooms and reproduce real-life situations in complete darkness. The "journey," which lasts about 75 minutes, takes place within the **Istituto dei Ciechi** (Institute for the Blind), not far from San Babila. Note: English speakers must fill a complete party of eight or bring a translator to go on this tour, and reservations are required.

Via Vivaio 7 • tel 02 76394478 • Closed Mon. • €€ • Metro: San Babila and Palestro, Line 1 • Bus: 54, 61, 94 • Tram: 9, 23, 29, 30

■ ATMosfera

To experience Milanese nightlife in motion, get on one of the two trams—ATMosfera1 or ATMosfera 2—that the Milan public transport company, known as ATM, has turned into restaurants. On board, a choice of three menus is served to 24 adventurous passengers. The trams leave from Piazza Castello (around Parco Sempione) at 8 p.m. and return after two hours of touring. Reservations are required.

Tel 02 48607607 • atm.it • €€€€

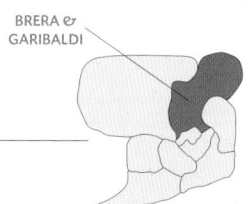

BRERA &
GARIBALDI

Brera & Garibaldi

Corso Garibaldi is perhaps the best place to get a sense of this part of Milan and its transformation over the centuries. While maintaining its popular character—with old *case di ringhiera* (apartment blocks with communal balconies), beautiful churches with red facades, and some timeless workshops—over the years the street has acquired more luxury window displays, culminating in the pedestrian-only Corso Como, where today's fashions are to be seen. The new Porta Nuova area is dominated by the sleek architecture of the UniCredit Tower. A similar transformation has taken place in artsy Brera, but despite the growing number of bars, restaurants, and shops, the area has retained the charm of the past. Here narrow streets and galleries such as the Accademia and Pinacoteca di Brera contribute to the bohemian atmosphere. It is particularly busy the third Sunday of the month, when some 50 vendors take over Via Fiori Chiari, Via Madonnina, and Via Formentini for a traditional antiques market.

◐ **"The Marriage of the Virgin," Raphael's masterpiece, has hung in the Pinacoteca di Brera since 1805.**

Brera & Garibaldi

The new, modern skyline of Milan rises up behind this quarter famous for its art and residential apartment blocks.

❶ Piazza del Carmine (see p. 100) Start your day at one of the most pleasant places in the city to stop and have a coffee, with a view of the neo-Gothic facade of Santa Maria del Carmine. When you're ready, walk down Via del Carmine, turning left on Via Brera.

❷ Pinacoteca di Brera (see pp. 106–107) Art has been taught and admired here since the late 18th century, with paintings by Caravaggio and others. Stroll in the Botanic Garden and visit the Observatory, then wander through the charming Brera district, home to the annual Design Week, down Via Brera, turning right on Via Pontaccio.

❸ Basilica di San Marco (see pp. 100–101) Take a step back in time at this church, founded by Eremitani monks in 1254. Here Mozart played during his stay in Milan, and Verdi performed his *Requiem* for the first time. Then backtrack down Via Pontaccio and turn right down Corso Garibaldi.

❽ Palazzo Lombardia (see p. 105) The new headquarters of the Lombardy Region since 2011, this congress hall includes a piazza with restaurants and impromptu dance parties on Saturday nights. The viewing terrace on the tower's 39th floor is open on Sundays.

VIA LUIGI GALVANI

Palazzo
Lombardia

❽

GIOIA

VIA GAETANO DE CASTILLIA

Stazione
Porta Garibaldi

VIALE LUIGI STURZO

VIA MELCHIORRE

❼ Piazza Gae
Aulenti

PIAZZA
EINAUDI

PORTA
NUOVA

VIA CARLO

7 Porta Nuova (see pp. 103–104) The UniCredit Tower and Piazza Gae Aulenti are but two symbols of this new city. Another is Palazzo Lombardia, reached by following the walkways to the Bosco Verticale, left on Via de Castillia and Via Restelli; or via Metro Garibaldi, Line 2 to Gioia.

6 Santa Maria Incoronata (see pp. 102–103) Take a rest from your walk at this double church, then move on to more secular pleasures down Corso Garibaldi, across Piazza XXV Aprile, and onto Corso Como, filled with shops and cafés. From here, access the high-rises of Porta Nuova by escalator.

5 Ponte delle Gabelle (see p. 102) This bridge, also known as the Conca dell'Incoronata, is where barges sailing along the Naviglio della Martesana had to stop and pay customs duties (*gabella*). Enjoy the view, then follow Via Marsala on your left until you reach Corso Garibaldi, and then turn left.

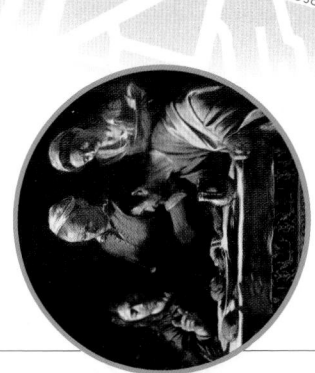

4 San Simpliciano (see p. 101) Founded by St. Ambrose, the church was completed by his successor, St. Simplician, who is buried here. After a visit to the 15th- and 16th-century cloisters continue on Corso Garibaldi, turning right on Via della Moscova and then left on Via San Marco to the bridge.

BRERA & GARIBALDI   DISTANCE: 2.4 MILES (3.8 KM)
TIME: ABOUT 7 HOURS METRO START: LANZA, LINE 2

0 ——— 200 meters
0 ——— 200 yards

Map labels: DE CRISTOFORIS · Ponte delle Gabelle · PIAZZA XXV APRILE · CORSO CASTELFIDARDO · MOSCOVA · Eataly Smeraldo · CORSO COMO · BASTIONI DI PORTA NUOVA · VIA MONTEBELLO · VIA GOITO · Basilica di San Marco · Santa Maria Incoronata · VIA MARSALA · VIA SAN MARCO · VIA DELLA MOSCOVA · VIA SOLFERINO · VIA BORGONUOVO · Pinacoteca di Brera · Museo del Risorgimento · San Simpliciano · PIAZZA SAN MARCO · VIA STATUTO · VIA PALERMO · VIA PONTACCIO · VIA FIORI CHIARI · Santa Maria del Carmine · Piazza del Carmine · CORSO GARIBALDI · VIA BRERA

The tripartite neo-Gothic facade of Santa Maria del Carmine, designed by Carlo Maciachini

Piazza del Carmine

1 Piazza del Carmine is a very special place for Milan, a corner of the city right in the charmingly trendy Brera district with its narrow streets and quirky shops. Enjoy a coffee outdoors at one of the many inviting café tables facing the redbrick, neo-Gothic facade of the church of **Santa Maria del Carmine.** In front of the church stands the striking bronze bust "The Great Tuscan" by the Polish sculptor Igor Mitoraj; next door is the flagship store of the American designer Marc Jacobs, which has a popular café.

Metro: Lanza, Line 2 • Bus: 57, 61

Pinacoteca di Brera

2 See pp. 106–107.

Via Brera 28 • tel 02 72263264 • Closed Mon., Jan. 1, May 1, Dec. 25 • €€€ • Metro: Lanza, Line 2 • Bus: 61 • Tram: 1, 4, 12, 14, 27

Basilica di San Marco

3 Founded in 1254 by the Order of Hermits of St. Augustine, this church has a musical vocation. The young Mozart actually lived in its rectory for three months, playing the organ as he wished. This favored instrument, built in 1564 by Benedict Antegnati, has now been declared a national monument. In another landmark event, the first performance of the *Requiem Mass* conducted by its composer Giuseppe Verdi on the first anniversary of Alessandro Manzoni's death also took place in this church, and it's easy to imagine the sacred music echoing through its three naves. According to legend, the church was dedicated to St. Mark to thank Venice for helping Milan in the struggle against Barbarossa. But the real hero of the basilica is St. Augustine, who appears in many of the church's artistic works, starting with the facade, where you will see statues of the saint accompanied by St. Ambrose and St. Mark, attributed to Giovanni di Balducci da Pisa (1320). The **sarcophagus** of the Blessed Lanfranco Settala is in the right transept, which also contains the frescoes by the brothers Giovanni Battista and Mauro della Rovere called "Fiammenghini." These show the institution of the Augustinian order by Pope Alexander IV. Among the most unusual works preserved at San Marco is a **nativity made of painted paper** in the mid-18th century by Francesco Londonio, painter and stage designer at La Scala in the time of Maria Theresa of Austria. While at the church, check outside for its posted schedule of classical music concerts (usually held Monday and Wednesday); they are worth a return visit as your time allows.

Piazza San Marco 1 • Metro: Lanza, Line 2

San Simpliciano

4 The church of San Simpliciano is a little hard to find, set back from Corso Garibaldi in a little square of old Milan. But the surprise is worth the detour. This is one of the four basilicas that, in the fourth century, St. Ambrose arranged to be built in the four corners of Milan when he became bishop of the city (the others are Sant'Ambrogio, San Nazaro, and San Dionigi, which has disappeared). Originally dedicated to the Virgin, the church was later dedicated to St. Simplician, successor of St. Ambrose. Unlike many others, this basilica has been little changed or restored, making it one of the most important examples of the Romanesque in Milan, as well as preserving much of its early Christian outside walls. The interior, with three naves of equal height, is filled with works of art, including in the apse a still vibrant fresco, "Coronation of the Virgin" by Ambrogio da Fossano, who was called "Bergognone."

Piazza San Simpliciano 7 • tel 02 862274 • Metro: Lanza, Line 2 • Bus: 61 • Tram: 4, 7, 12, 14

IN **THE KNOW**

Eataly Smeraldo (*eataly .net*) opened in Milan near Porta Nuova at no. 10 Piazza XXV Aprile in early 2014, to immediate success. Its 54,000 square feet (5,000 sq m) devoted to shops and restaurants include three food floors dominated by a large stage hosting a full program of concerts, a tribute to the origins of the location, the historic Smeraldo Theater.

GOOD **EATS**

■ CARMINIO
Pleasant and friendly without giving in to fashion, Adele Prosdocimi's restaurant is a safe haven of well-executed dishes prepared with fresh ingredients. **Via del Carmine 3, tel 02 72022992, closed Sun., €€€**

■ PISACCO
Quality at affordable prices and in a modern and fashionable surrounding: These are the ingredients of the success of Andrea Berton's bistro in the heart of the Brera district. **Via Solferino 48, tel 02 91765472, closed Mon., €€€**

■ RIGOLO
This has been a second home for journalists of the *Corriere della Sera* since 1958 (the headquarters of the newspaper is just steps away). The kitchen is traditional and precise, and the service is always professional and courteous. **Via Solferino 11, cnr. Largo Treves, tel 02 86463220, closed Mon., €€€€**

Ponte delle Gabelle

5 This hidden gem, a bit out of the way, is a wonderful place to sit and imagine how Milan used to be when the Navigli still flowed around the city and barges laden with goods sailed from the countryside into the bustling center. Also known as the Conca dell'Incoronata, this is the only urban part left of the Naviglio della Martesana, the last surviving bridge of the waterway and the last gate. This masterpiece of hydraulic engineering dates from 1496 and the rule of Ludovico il Moro, created to regulate the waters of the Naviglio della Martesana. It is said to have been designed by Leonardo da Vinci. The canal, commissioned by Francesco Sforza, connected Milan to Bergamo and the barges in transit were required to pay an excise duty known as the *gabella*. The great stock market crash year of 1929 also struck the Ponte delle Gabelle, the Bridge of Taxes, as that was the year the canals were covered and the watery link between Via San Marco and Via Castelfidardo finally ceased its activity.

Via San Marco 45 • Metro: Moscova, Line 2 • Bus: 43, 61

Santa Maria Incoronata

6 At first glance, it looks as if you are seeing double, and indeed the facade of the church of Santa Maria Incoronata is a double one. This 15th-century masterpiece was formed by merging two churches. The one dedicated to Santa Maria in Garegnano was built by the

Eremitani (Hermit Fathers) of San Marco, while the other was built in 1450 by Bianca Maria Visconti, wife of Francesco Sforza, in honor of San Nicola da Tolentino. The square church was combined in 1468, and offers a welcome respite from the shopping and crowds of the lively area between Corso Garibaldi and Corso Como. Within, the six chapels of the Incoronata contain many masterpieces, including, in the first chapel of the left nave,"The Mystic Torch," a fresco by Bergognone depicting a fairly rare subject. Do not miss the **cloister,** where the influence of Filarete can be seen, and the **Humanist Library** with three naves from 1487, recently reopened after a long restoration.

Corso Garibaldi 116 • tel 02 654855 • Metro: Moscova, Line 2 • Bus: 37, 43, 70, 94 • Tram: 2, 4, 7

Porta Nuova

7 "How beautiful the city is, how large the city is … with ever higher skyscrapers and so many cars, always more, always more, always more!" These exuberant words are the translation of a favorite Italian

Escalator to Piazza Gae Aulenti, with the UniCredit Tower in the background

song of Giorgio Gaber dating from 1969, when the areas of Garibaldi, Varesine, and Isola were not connected to one another. Yet they speak of the Porta Nuova development, which, together with City Life, is the city's largest urban renewal project since World War II. Covering nearly 72 acres (29 ha), this vertical steel-and-glass district has grown up since 2007 just a few steps away from the city center, boldly changing the city's skyline.

This is a place where businesses, restaurants, and bars coexist side by side, making this sleek and modern setting a favorite after-work hangout among the Milanese. Visit in the late afternoon to see the pink sky reflected in the water of the fountains and against the glassy facades. Sit in lovely **Piazza Gae Aulenti,** raised like a stage above street level, and crane your neck looking up at the spire of the **UniCredit Tower,** designed by Cesar Pelli, an architect known for building high towers. Indeed, this is the tallest of three skyscrapers built here, near Stazione Porta Garibaldi and Corso Como; its height of 758 feet (231 m) also makes it the tallest building in Italy. Not far away is the **Torre Diamante,** designed by the Kohn Pederson Fox Associates studio. Though not particularly tall at 450 feet (137 m), its unusual beveled shape (thus the name *diamante,* or diamond) has quickly made it a landmark.

Students of modern architecture will also want to note the two **Bosco Verticale** (Vertical Wood) buildings by architect Stefano Boeri. These skyscrapers are models of sustainable residential buildings, their terraces planted with some 900 trees and close to 2,000 plants, all to aid in creating a microclimate, absorb CO_2, and produce oxygen.

IN **THE KNOW**

Not far from Porta Nuova is the pedestrian Corso Como, joining Garibaldi Station with Piazza XXV Aprile as another of Milan's famous shopping streets and very lively at night. Worth a visit is **10 Corso Como** (see p. 110; *10corsocomo* *.com*), opened by Carla Sozzani, an art collector and sister of *Vogue Italia*'s editor in chief. This is a fashion store plus art gallery, bookshop, restaurant, and luxury B&B, all within a picturesque Milan courtyard.

Metro: Gioia, Line 2; Centrale F. S., Line 2, 3; Garibaldi F. S., Line 2, 5

On a clear day you can see the Alps from the Palazzo Lombardia tower.

Palazzo Lombardia

8 On the edges of the new Porta Nuova neighborhood, the Palazzo Lombardia has been the headquarters of the Lombardy regional government since 2011. Designed by New York architectural studio **Pei, Cobb, Freed & Partners,** the complex includes a tower 528 feet (161 m) high (second in height only to the UniCredit Tower) that houses the regional committee and the presidential offices, and four lower buildings arranged in a sinusoidal pattern enclosing a covered square. If you're here on a Saturday night, you may find yourself at an impromptu dance party, free and fun for all. For another chance to take your breath away, you can access the observation deck on the tower's 39th floor every Sunday from 10 a.m. to 6 p.m. From here you can enjoy a wonderful view of Milan, all the way to the Alps. Entry is free, but be prepared to wait in line.

Piazza Città di Lombardia 1 • tel 800 318318 • regione.lombardia.it • Metro: Gioia, Line 2; Centrale F. S., Line 2, 3 • Bus: 43, 82 • Passante railway: Repubblica and Garibaldi

Pinacoteca di Brera

This is one of northern Italy's greatest art galleries, filled with Lombard, Venetian, and other masterpieces from across the centuries.

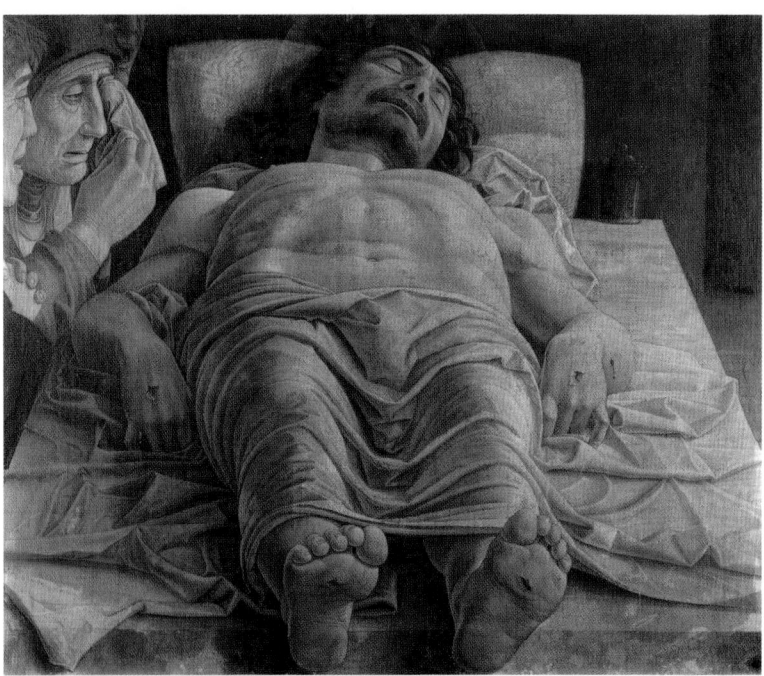

Mantegna's "Lamentation of Christ" came to the Brera through the mediation of Antonio Canova.

The Brera, as it is called, dates from the 1700s, and its art was intended to help inform students of the adjoining arts academy. Over the years bequests, purchases, and the efforts of Napoleon—who used the gallery to exhibit art plundered from across Italy—have made it one of the best collections in Europe.

■ THE PALAZZO

Before entering the gallery, take in its home, the **Palazzo Brera.** Parts of the structure date back to the 12th century, but architect Francesco Maria Richini—who was also responsible for the Ca' Granda's Cortile Maggiore (see p. 91)—designed most of the present building after 1650 as a college, botanical garden, and astronomical observatory for the Jesuits. The gallery comprises a lobby with eight detached frescoes from 1487, and then proceeds in roughly chronological order through 38 rooms.

■ ROOMS 2–15

The Brera is most celebrated for works by northern Italian painters from the 13th to 16th centuries, and those of Venice in particular, but as early as rooms 2 and 3 you will find masterpieces from across Italy, notably panels by the Sienese artists Ambrogio Lorenzetti and Andrea di Bartolo. Room 4, by contrast, has paintings by Gentile da Fabriano, one of the greatest painters from the Marche region in central Italy. In the following rooms are a wealth of sublime, mostly Venetian paintings from Alvise Vivarini, Vittorio Carpaccio, Titian, Cima da Conegliano, and Giovanni and Gentile

SAVVY **TRAVELER**

Hidden within the Palazzo di Brera, the **Orto Botanico,** or Botanic Garden (entrance also from Via Gabba 10) is one of the most poetic spots in the city. Created on the orders of Maria Theresa of Austria, it encompasses an area of just over an acre (0.5 ha) with many old trees as well as special collections, including medicinal plants, sages, and spring bulbs.

Bellini, as well as the "Lamentation of Christ" (1480) by Andrea Mantegna.

■ ROOMS 16–38

A number of the names in the second half of the gallery may be less familiar, but rooms 16 to 19 allow you to explore some of the painters most closely associated with Lombardy, notably Bernardino Luini and Vincenzo Foppa. Other fine, if less celebrated, central Italian painters include Carlo Crivelli, Luca Signorelli, and Niccolò Alunno. More famous names return in room 24: Raphael and his outstanding "The Marriage of the Virgin" (ca 1504), and Caravaggio, whose famous "Supper at Emmaus" (1606) is usually hung in room 29.

BRERA & GARIBALDI

Via Brera 28 • tel 02 92800361 (tickets) or 02 72263264 (switchboard) • brera.beniculturali.it • Online tickets vivaticket.it • Closed Mon., Jan. 1, May 1, Dec. 25 • €€€ • Metro: Lanza, Line 2 • Bus: 61 • Tram: 1, 4, 12, 14, 27

Music in Milan

Music in Milan is associated primarily with opera and La Scala (see pp. 62–63), but the city's musical heritage has much older and richer roots. In the fourth century St. Ambrose composed hymns, some of which survive, that laid the foundations for early church plainchant, and in later centuries composers such as Mozart and Giuseppe Verdi flocked to the city attracted by its patrons and cultural stature. Today, numerous churches, festivals, and venues host a range of classical, chamber, jazz, and other performances.

Performers at the annual Piano City music festival, when more than 300 piano concerts are held across the city over three days in May. Opposite: Auditorium di Milano, home to the celebrated Orchestra La Verdi.

Mozart in Milan

Mozart was just 13 when he made the first of three Italian journeys in the years 1769 to 1773, each of which involved extended periods in Milan. Accompanied by his father, Leopold, he first lodged in San Marco's rectory (see p. 100) in January 1770, and was commissioned by Karl Joseph von Firmian, an Austrian count based in the city, to write an opera, *Mitridate*. Mozart may also have begun his Symphony No. 10 in G (K. 71) at the same time. *Mitridate* received its first performance, with the composer conducting from the keyboard, in December 1770 at the Teatro Regio Ducal, then the city's main opera house (La Scala was inaugurated eight years later). Another opera (*Ascanio in Alba*) and the Symphony No. 13 in F (K. 112) appeared during a second Milanese visit in 1771. A third visit in 1772–1773 produced yet another opera (*Lucio Silla*), several string quartets, and the famous motet *Exsultate jubilate*.

Verdi in Milan

The Milanese praised young Mozart, but the reception afforded Giuseppe Verdi (1813–1901), one of Italy's finest composers, was decidedly more muted. Verdi was born outside of Milan, but in 1832 moved here to be in northern Italy's cultural heart. His application to the music conservatory was rejected; his piano playing, among other things, considered substandard. In 1900, when he had achieved worldwide fame, he was asked if the conservatory might be renamed in his honor. He refused: "They did not want me in my youth," he said. "They will not have me in my old age." (It took his name anyway.) After 1839, and the performance of his first opera, *Oberto, Conte di San Bonifacio,* at La Scala, he began to prosper. La Scala premiered several subsequent operas, while San Marco (see p. 100) saw the first performance of his *Requiem* in 1874. Verdi would die (and was buried) in Milan; the street outside his hotel (Via Mazzini) was famously covered with straw so that the sound of carriages would not disturb the dying composer.

MORE **MUSIC**

Casa Castello Sforzesco Summer classical concerts in the castle courtyards (amicidellamusicamilano.it)

Santa Maria della Passione Often hosts organ recitals (Via Conservatorio 14, tel 02 76021370)

Teatro dal Verme Evening concerts and smaller afternoon recitals (Via San Giovanni sul Muro 2, tel 02 87905)

Pop, Jazz, and Rock Visit vivimilano.corriere.it/concerti for current listings of shows.

BRERA & GARIBALDI

Concept Stores

Concept stores are retail shops designed to provide patrons with a particular experience—clothes, furnishings, walls, and merchandise tailored to present a unified story to a specific segment of the population, whether high fashion, minimalistic, or hipster. These stores are an alternative to staid boutiques, presenting a variety of products that represent a targeted lifestyle.

■ SHOPPING POSTINDUSTRIAL

High Tech (*Piazza XXV Aprile 12, tel 02 6241101*), in the Brera and Garibaldi area, is synonymous with a Milan concept store. Opened in 1982, High Tech has always followed the principles of functionality, aesthetics, and reasonable price. Relax on the upper floor among sofas, armchairs, tables, chairs, and bookcases, while the ground floor encourages browsing through perfumes, stationery, and fashion accessories. Down a few steps brings you to everything for the kitchen and bathroom, all with the same feel. Far from the city center, **Cargo** (*Via Meucci 39, tel 02 2722131*) has enchanted shoppers since opening in 2001 in the vast former Ovomaltina factory. Here you have the impression of entering into the hold of a ship loaded with goods of all kinds. In addition to furniture from places such as China, Morocco, India, and Indochina there are furnishings, kitchen accessories, books, and gadgets.

■ ECLECTIC TASTES

A former journalist and fashion expert, Carla Sozzani is the mastermind behind **10 Corso Como** (*Corso Como 10, tel 02 29002674, 10corsocomo.com*), the concept store opened in 1991 in a former garage that changed the look of the street of Garibaldi forever. The space mixes art, books, fashion, and design objects selected according to the taste and sensibility of its creator. Don't miss the photography exhibitions held in the **Galleria Carla Sozzani,** on the first floor, and stop in the design-focused bookstore nearby. In the Magenta area, another personality has created a space devoted to fashion and design and lent her name to the store: **Rossana Orlandi** (*Via Matteo Bandello 14/16, tel 02 467447, rossanaorlandi.com*). Here she transformed a former 19th-century tie factory into an apparently chaotic but actually well-orchestrated world containing unique pieces, limited editions

Galleria Carla Sozzani, devoted to photography, art, design, and architecture

by established creative artists, and objects tracked down from all over the globe: from "burned" tables by Maarten Bass to furniture made from recycled wood by Piet Hein Eek. The restaurant next door, **Marta,** was designed by Paola Navone, whose furniture and accessories can be bought in the nearby gallery.

■ FASHION AND DESIGN

Around the Giardini Pubblici, it is worth seeking out the **JVstore** *(Via Melzo 7, tel 02 205231)*, devoted to design and fashion by Jannelli & Volpi, the historic Italian wallpaper company. To reach this concept store you need to go into the company's showroom and climb a flight of stairs. It will not disappoint; the selection is always varied and unusual, with well-chosen Italian, French, and Scandinavian designs and some fashion, including clothes by Marimekko. The same love of the chase is to be found back in the Magenta area at **Wait and See** *(Via Santa Marta 14, tel 02 72080195)*, the store of Uberta Zambeletti, a fashion designer and interior decorator with a cosmopolitan soul. Within this former convent in the historic center, you will find clothing, accessories, jewelry, objects, stationery, and original vintage pieces from all over the world.

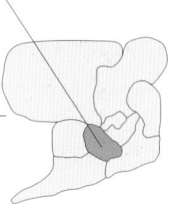

Torre Velasca to Piazza Affari

From the top of Torre Velasca at 348 feet (106 m) high you can see what was the heart of the city in the Middle Ages. To this day the streets close to Piazza dei Mercanti are still named after the merchants, coinmakers, and craftsmen who enlivened Milan and enriched it, setting up financial businesses in this area, from the ancient Moneta to the modern stock exchange. It was no coincidence that in the 15th century the Borromeo family, having grown enormously rich through banking, decided to build their own palazzo here. Carlo and Federico, both St. Ambrose's enlightened successors at the head of the Milan diocese, also lived in the Palazzo Borromeo. The great patron Federico founded the Biblioteca Ambrosiana and the Pinacoteca Ambrosiana, cultural landmarks of Milan and the main destinations in this section.

◐ **Torre Velasca
and the heart of
medieval Milan**

Torre Velasca to Piazza Affari

Wander the heart of medieval Milan, where streets are still named after the ancient trades and guilds.

6 The Ambrosiana (see pp. 122–123) Allow plenty of time for one of the oldest art galleries (*pinacoteca*) in the world and its library, founded by Cardinal Federico Borromeo in 1607. Walk around the pinacoteca down Via dell'Ambrosiana.

7 Casa Museo Mangini Bonomi (see pp. 118–119) People's lives are described by this collection of common objects. Walk to the back of the pinacoteca to the square.

8 San Sepolcro (see pp. 119–120) This church was rebuilt after the First Crusade in the shape of the Holy Sepulchre in Jerusalem. After a visit, head down Via del Bollo and turn left on Via Santa Maria Podone.

9 Palazzo Borromeo (see pp. 120–121) If it's open, wander this late Gothic palace with its superb games room and wonderful frescoes. Next backtrack down Via Santa Maria Podone, turn left on Via Santa Maria Fulcorina, and continue to Piazza Affari.

10 Palazzo Mezzanotte (see p. 121) Dominating Piazza Affari, this imposing building was until 1987 headquarters of the Milan stock exchange.

TORRE VELASCA TO PIAZZA AFFARI   DISTANCE: 0.8 MILE (1.3 KM) TIME: ABOUT 5 HOURS   METRO START: MISSORI, LINE 3

Map labels: VIA MERAVIGLI · Palazzo Mezzanotte · 10 · VIA G. NEGRI · PIAZZA AFFARI · Poste Centrali · VIA SANTA MARIA FULCORINA · VIA DELLA POSTA · VIA BORROMEI · Santa Maria Podone · Palazzo Borromeo 9 · VIA S. MARIA PODONE · VIA SANT'ORSOLA · VIA SAN MAURILIO · VIA FOSSE ARDEATINE · VIA SANTA MARTA · VIA NERINO · San Giorgio al Palazzo

TORRE VELASCA TO PIAZZA AFFARI

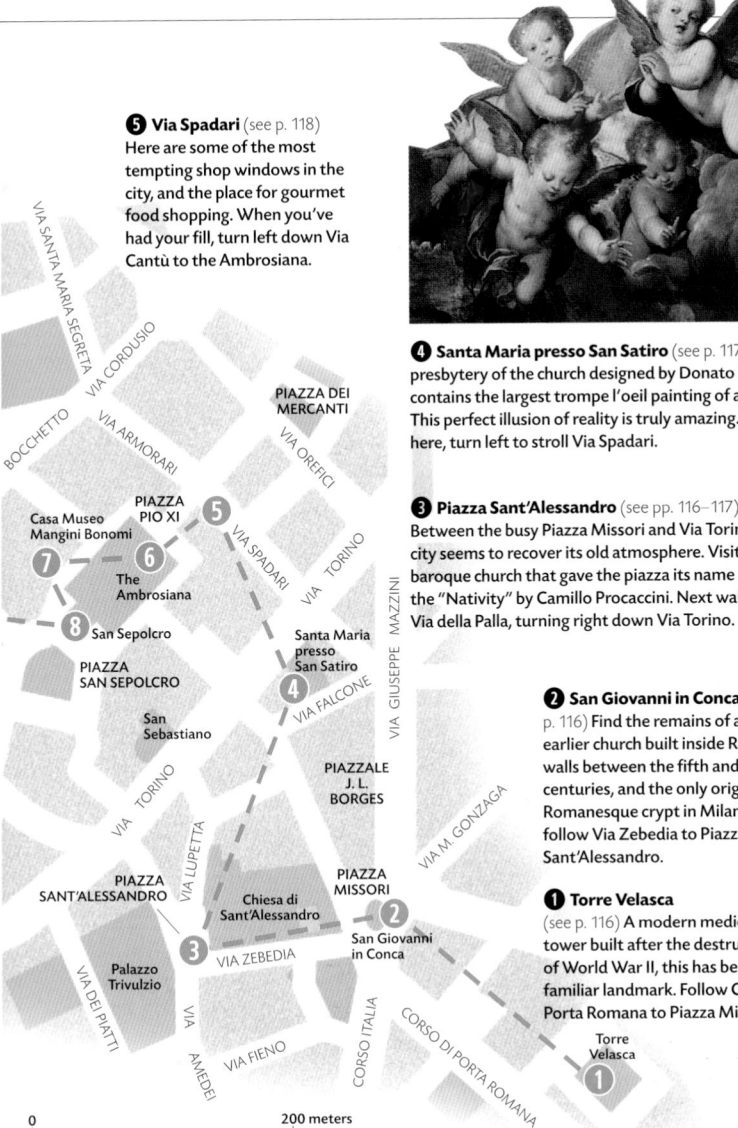

5 **Via Spadari** (see p. 118) Here are some of the most tempting shop windows in the city, and the place for gourmet food shopping. When you've had your fill, turn left down Via Cantù to the Ambrosiana.

4 **Santa Maria presso San Satiro** (see p. 117) The presbytery of the church designed by Donato Bramante contains the largest trompe l'oeil painting of all time. This perfect illusion of reality is truly amazing. From here, turn left to stroll Via Spadari.

3 **Piazza Sant'Alessandro** (see pp. 116–117) Between the busy Piazza Missori and Via Torino the city seems to recover its old atmosphere. Visit the baroque church that gave the piazza its name and see the "Nativity" by Camillo Procaccini. Next walk along Via della Palla, turning right down Via Torino.

2 **San Giovanni in Conca** (see p. 116) Find the remains of an earlier church built inside Roman walls between the fifth and sixth centuries, and the only original Romanesque crypt in Milan. Then follow Via Zebedia to Piazza Sant'Alessandro.

1 **Torre Velasca** (see p. 116) A modern medieval tower built after the destruction of World War II, this has become a familiar landmark. Follow Corso di Porta Romana to Piazza Missori.

Map labels:
VIA SANTA MARIA SEGRETA
VIA CORDUSIO
BOCCHETTO
VIA ARMORARI
PIAZZA DEI MERCANTI
VIA OREFICI
Casa Museo Mangini Bonomi
7
PIAZZA PIO XI
5
VIA SPADARI
VIA TORINO
6
The Ambrosiana
8 San Sepolcro
PIAZZA SAN SEPOLCRO
Santa Maria presso San Satiro
4
VIA FALCONE
VIA GIUSEPPE MAZZINI
San Sebastiano
VIA TORINO
PIAZZALE J. L. BORGES
VIA M. GONZAGA
VIA DI PORTA ROMANA
PIAZZA SANT'ALESSANDRO
VIA LUPETTA
Chiesa di Sant'Alessandro
PIAZZA MISSORI
2 San Giovanni in Conca
3
VIA ZEBEDIA
Palazzo Trivulzio
VIA DEI PIATTI
VIA AMEDEI
VIA FIENO
CORSO ITALIA
CORSO DI PORTA ROMANA
Torre Velasca
1

0 — 200 meters
0 — 200 yards

The Torre Velasca, which takes its name from the Spanish governor Juan Fernandez de Velasco, stands in a piazza of the same name.

Torre Velasca

1 Built between 1956 and 1958 to symbolize Milan's modernism, the Torre Velasca's unusual "mushroom" shape has been compared to a medieval watchtower. It is a local landmark, with a height of 348 feet (106 m); the first 18 floors are offices while the remaining 7 are occupied by apartments.

Piazza Velasca 5 • Metro: Missori, Line 3 • Bus: 12, 15, 27

San Giovanni in Conca

2 This church began in a residential Roman area in the early Christian era, was rebuilt in the 11th century, destroyed by Barbarossa, and rebuilt several more times until it was deconsecrated by the Austrians and shut down by the French. The Waldensians, who bought the building, moved the whole facade to Via Francesco Sforza and incorporated it into their new church in 1950. Although this is something to see, San Giovanni in Conca's great treasure is still back in Piazza Missori, 1,100 yards (1 km) away. There you will find part of the apse and the crypt, both dating from the 4th to 11th centuries, the latter in which Roman and medieval remains can be seen. It is the only original Romanesque crypt still in Milan.

Piazza Missori • Closed Sun.–Mon. • Metro: Missori, Line 3 • Tram: 12, 15, 27

Piazza Sant'Alessandro

3 Even though some may hold that Milan lacks attractive public squares, the Piazza Sant'Alessandro is a pleasant exception. Overlooked by the dome of the **Chiesa di Sant'Alessandro,** it is a harmonious, baroque corner of the city. The church was built by the Barnabites in 1601 to plans by Lorenzo Binago and then Richini, and it follows their classic layout of a central plan with a dome and a baroque facade flanked by two bell towers. The church is dedicated to St. Alexander, who may (or may not) have been imprisoned there. Wander inside to see the fine wooden pulpit embedded with precious stones, as well as many works by area artists dating from the 17th and 18th centuries. Be sure to look for the three masterpieces by Camillo Procaccini: "Nativity," "Assumption," and "Crucifixion With the Madonna and St. John." Next door is the late baroque building of the **Scuole Arcimbolde,** founded by the Barnabites and now used by the state university. Opposite the church rises the simple facade of the **Palazzo Trivulzio,** built in the 18th century to plans by the architect Giovanni Ruggeri. Peek through to the internal courtyard at the decorated gateway made of white and red marble. It was moved here from the elaborate Palazzo Mozzanica before that was demolished to make room for Corso Vittorio Emanuele.

Piazza Sant'Alessandro • Metro: Missori, Line 3 • Tram: 12, 15, 27

Santa Maria presso San Satiro

4 Perhaps the most stunning church in Milan lies behind the busy Via Torino, easy to miss unless you are looking for it. But once you do go inside, you will be impressed at how imposing and large it seems, thanks to the skill of its architect, Donato Bramante. When he was commissioned, in the late 15th century, to build a church on this very small site, Bramante still wanted to achieve a monumental effect. He used a Latin cross plan, with a chancel that is actually only three feet (91 cm) deep. See for yourself how it all looks much larger, thanks to Bramante's clever use of trompe l'oeil behind the altar and in a false choir. The octagonal baptistry, reached from the right aisle, is beautifully decorated with putti and male busts with a 16th-century font at its center.

Via Torino 17–19 • tel 02 874683 • Closed Mon. • Metro: Duomo, Line 1, 3 • Tram: 2, 3, 4, 12, 14, 19, 20, 24, 27

IN **THE KNOW**

On Sunday mornings from 8 a.m. to 1 p.m. four streets— Via Armorari, Via Cordusio, Via Cesare Cantù, and Galleria Cordusio—are lined with vendors in a traditional Borsino market for those seeking stamps, coins, and postcards. First held in 1938, this gathering near the Ambrosiana has become the benchmark for enthusiasts who come to buy, sell, and swap.

Via Spadari

5 In the Middle Ages, the workshops and houses of merchants belonging to different guilds were located in this area, where the best delicatessens in Milan are to be found today. It is really hard to walk along Via Spadari and Via Victor Hugo without giving in to temptation. Approaching from Via Torino, on your left at no. 9 will be the oldest of the city's delicatessens, here since 1883—**Peck,** with its wine shop and restaurant. At no. 4 on the opposite side of the street is the fish shop **Pescheria Spadari,** established in 1933, next to the pastel colors of **Ladurée** *(no. 6)* with its macarons and, the most recent arrival, the concept store **Noberasco1908,** devoted to the art of dried fruits. Around the corner on Via Victor Hugo are two city landmarks, the starred **Ristorante Cracco** *(Via Victor Hugo 4, tel 02 876774, closed Sun., €€€€€),* next to the historic shop of **Giovanni Galli,** at no. 2. You can't go wrong in treating yourself at either establishment. The latter, founded in Porta Romana in 1911, is deservedly well known for its marrons glacés, fondants, *boeri* (liqueur chocolates filled with whole cherries), and pralines.

Metro: Duomo, Line 1, 3 • Tram: 1, 2, 3, 12, 14, 16, 24, 27

The Ambrosiana

6 See pp. 122–123.

Piazza Pio XI 2 • tel 02 806921 • Closed Mon., Jan. 1, Easter Sun., Dec. 25 • €€€ • Metro: Cordusio, Line 1 • Tram: 2, 4, 5, 12, 14, 16, 19, 20, 24, 27

Casa Museo Mangini Bonomi

7 The everyday life of ordinary people through the ages may perhaps be best described through the household items and other things each era put to common use. You can try this theory out thanks to the eclectic collection gathered by Emilio Carlo Mangini, now displayed on five floors of a 15th-century palazzo next to the Ambrosiana. There are hundreds of things to see, ranging from trunks to playing cards, from magic lanterns to keys, from weapons to archaeological finds, forming a real tribute to the pleasure of collecting.

Via dell'Ambrosiana 20 • tel 02 86451455 • museomanginibonomi.it • Tours by reservation only on Mon., Wed., Thurs. • Metro: Cordusio, Line 1 • Tram: 12, 14, 16

San Sepolcro

8 In 1030 Benedetto Ronzone, master of the Zecca (mint) of Milan, built this church dedicated to the Holy Trinity near his house. One of his descendants, returning from the First Crusade, rebuilt the church to imitate the Church of the Holy Sepulchre in Jerusalem. This was one of its many reconstructions, but what we see today is the result of a return to the Romanesque Lombard style in the late 19th century, with its redbrick facade between a bell tower and a clock tower. However, Santo Sepolcro's finest period was in the

Part of the collection of objects at the eclectic Casa Museo Mangini Bonomi

16th century, when Carlo Borromeo made the church the head-quarters of the Oblati di Sant'Ambrogio (and of San Carlo since 1611). Vivid polychromatic terra-cotta scenes depict such events as Christ washing his disciples' feet and Peter's denial. Be sure to visit the large, original **crypt,** which runs the whole length of the church, covered by marble slabs from the paving of the Roman Forum. Once back outside, take a look at the balcony opposite the church. This is where Mussolini made his first public address in 1919, an event that is interpreted by many as the birth of fascism.

Piazza San Sepolcro • tel 02 874685 • Metro: Cordusio, Line 1; Duomo, Line 1, 3 • Bus: 50, 54 • Tram: 2, 3, 12, 14, 19, 27

Palazzo Borromeo

9 Still owned by the ancient family of the two archbishops Carlo and Federico Borromeo and rarely open to the public, this private palazzo was built in the late 14th century, when the

The honor yard of Palazzo Borromeo has three porticoed sides with pointed arches.

noble family arrived in Milan. The massive palace was extended and rebuilt several times over the centuries, then seriously damaged during World War II (although rebuilt as accurately as possible). Set in the 17th-century brick facade is the beautiful 15th-century **ogival doorway,** above which spreads the Borromeo family crest, a resting dromedary. In the second courtyard of the palace is the **Sala dei Giochi** (games room) with Gothic frescoes of international renown. Among them is "Il Gioco dei Tarocchi" ("The Game of Tarot") depicting five characters playing cards beneath three pomegranate trees.

Piazza Borromeo 12 • Metro: Cordusio, Line 1

Palazzo Mezzanotte

10 Boldly placed in front of the city's stock exchange, Maurizio Cattelan's statue titled **L.O.V.E.**—standing for *libertà, odio, vendetta, eternità* (liberty, hatred, revenge, eternity)—is one of Milan's most controversial works of art. It's easy to understand why, and to interpret for yourself the symbolism of a huge Carrara marble hand with the middle finger making a defiant gesture. It faces the vast Palazzo Mezzanotte, built between 1928 and 1932 for the Milan stock exchange on the site of a Roman theater. Look on the building's facade for a marble slab depicting a plan of the ruins. Inside, a stained-glass ceiling shows the sky and its constellations and allows daylight onto the huge trading floor, now used for conferences. Piazza Affari affords fun people-watching, as passersby absorb the meaning of the great hand.

Piazza Affari 6 • tel 02 80287554 • museomanginibonomi.it • Metro: Cordusio, Line 1 • Tram: 1, 2, 3, 4, 12, 14, 24, 16

GOOD **EATS**

■ **ALLA COLLINA PISTOIESE**
Pasta with beans, *bistecca Fiorentina* (thick T-bone steak grilled over charcoal), *castagnaccio* (chestnut flour cake). This restaurant has served authentic Tuscan cuisine since 1938. **Via Amedei 1, tel 02 86451085, €€€€**

■ **LA VECCHIA LATTERIA**
This historic vegetarian "latteria" is always busy and crowded. It's open for lunch and until 10 p.m. Tues. and Thurs. for *eppi auar* (happy hour), Milan's tasty version of the *aperitivo.* **Via dell'Unione 6, tel 02 874401, closed Sun., €€**

■ **OTTIMOMASSIMO**
From breakfast to aperitivo, this gourmet restaurant in the fine-dining area of downtown Milan offers an amazing range of savory sandwiches, soups, salads, and desserts prepared using high-quality ingredients served in a minimalist two-story setting. **Via Victor Hugo 3, tel 02 49457661, closed Sun., €€**

The Ambrosiana

Beautiful period rooms and many superb works make this library and picture gallery two of Milan's most important cultural attractions.

"Basket of Fruit" by Caravaggio, one of the masterpieces of the Pinacoteca Ambrosiana

In 1607 Cardinal Federico Borromeo, the archbishop of Milan, founded the Biblioteca Ambrosiana, one of the world's first public libraries, and the Pinacoteca Ambrosiana, Milan's oldest gallery, as part of his belief that art and learning were a means of spreading the Christian faith. The cardinal's own private collection—172 paintings in all—formed the basis of the *pinacoteca,* but he dispatched agents to scour Europe for more works of art. Today the gallery can draw on more than 1,500 paintings for its walls, displayed in chronological order across 24 rooms.

■ THE PINACOTECA

Many of the gallery's most celebrated paintings are in the first six rooms, starting in room 1 with Titian's vibrant **"Adoration of the Magi"** (1559–1560). Rooms 2 and 3 usually contain some of the key Renaissance works from outside Borromeo's original collection, notably a brooding **"Portrait of a Musician"** (ca 1490) attributed to Leonardo da Vinci and the delicate **"Madonna del Padiglione"** (1493) by Sandro Botticelli (*padiglione* in Italian means "pavilion," after the red canopy above the Madonna). Rooms 5 and 6 contain Raphael's cartoon (1509) for his painting of "The School of Athens," now in the Vatican, and Caravaggio's **"Basket of Fruit"** (1599) one of the finest still lifes in Italian painting. Other paintings to look out for in these early rooms include works by the Milanese artist Bernardino Luini (ca 1480–1532), notably **"The Holy Family"** with St. Anne and a young John the Baptist, and the large fresco **"Christ Crowned With Thorns."** Subsequent rooms contain Flemish works, historical artifacts, and works by later Italian artists.

IN **THE KNOW**

Don't miss some of the ruins of the ancient Roman city of Milan, including parts of the original forum, discovered during restoration of the Biblioteca Ambrosiana in the 1990s. Tickets for the site (which is beneath and entered from the *pinacoteca*) are available at the pinacoteca ticket office, with a reduction if combined with the gallery.

■ THE BIBLIOTECA

The Biblioteca Ambrosiana has a million printed books, 36,000 manuscripts in Italian, Latin, Greek, and Arabic, and 12,000 drawings. Its highlight is the **Codex Atlanticus,** Leonardo da Vinci's collection of papers and drawings, covering the whole life of the Renaissance genius. It consists of 1,119 pages, a selection of which can be seen in rotation in 22 display cases in the **Sala Federiciana,** the library's ancient reading room. Other exhibits include autographed manuscripts by Galileo, Machiavelli, and Thomas Aquinas, as well as classical works annotated by famous Italian writers such as Petrarch and Boccaccio.

TORRE VELASCA TO PIAZZA AFFARI

Piazza Pio XI 2 • tel 02 806921 • www.ambrosiana.eu • Pinacoteca closed Mon., Jan. 1, Easter Sun., Dec. 25; Biblioteca closed Sat.–Sun. *&* periods Dec.–Jan. *&* July–Aug. • €€€ • Metro: Cordusio, Line 1 • Tram: 2, 4, 5, 12, 14, 16, 19, 20, 24, 27

Milanese Cuisine

Milan's location on rich agricultural plains close to the mountains melds well with its culinary heritage that includes staples of peasant cooking from centuries past and the influences of its Spanish and Austrian invaders. All this results in a range of food and wine broad even by Italian standards.

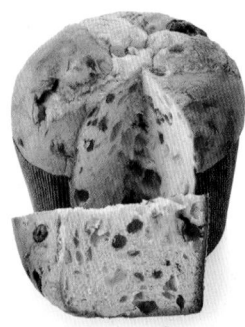

The sweet Italian dessert bread panettone (above) began in Milan, but the city's signature dish remains *risotto alla Milanese* (opposite), often flavored with saffron and bone marrow.

The Cult of Risotto

The mountains north of Milan yield many foodstuffs, including cheeses and the distinctive *bresaola della Valtellina,* thinly sliced air-dried beef often served with lemon juice and black pepper as an antipasto (hors d'oeuvre). But it is the plains that have had the most profound effect on the city's cuisine. Pasta is found in the Milanese restaurants, but the introduction of rice to Lombardy in the 14th century, and the fact that the flatlands of the Po River are easily flooded to create rice paddies, means that *riso,* or rice, and in particular **risotto,** a 19th-century creation, is a far more popular staple. While risotto comes in many versions, the classic *risotto alla Milanese* relies on saffron (introduced here by the Spanish) for its distinctive golden hue and subtle flavor. Also popular is **polenta,** once the dish of the poorest of the poor and made from spelt or millet; it is now usually based on cornmeal.

The Main Event

Risotto is often eaten as a primo, or the first course of a meal, perhaps after an antipasto. The main course, or secondo, follows, and in Milan might typically

involve **bollito,** a type of slow-cooked stew
with meats and vegetables, often with *mostarda*
(mustard mixed with candied fruit) or a classic
salsa verde (a "green" sauce of garlic, oil, anchovies,
and parsley). Another popular stew, **cassoeula,**
is made with pork and cabbage. Equally hearty is
osso buco, one of the great Lombard dishes, made
from veal shank browned in butter and cooked
in wine. A lighter veal alternative is **cotoletta alla
Milanese,** a breaded fillet fried in butter. Similar
to Austria's Wiener schnitzel, locals claim this is
their own invention, dating from the 12th century.
Other regional staples—such **trippa alla Milanese,** tripe with either tomatoes or
white beans—require stronger stomachs.

LOCAL **CHEESE**

Local and Alpine cheeses can be a
delicious part of any Milanese meal.

Crescza A popular soft, white,
rindless *stracchino*

Gorgonzola Part of the stracchino
family of cheeses, made from the milk
of cows "tired" *(stracche)* after their
long walk from summer pastures

Marscapone This cream cheese is a
key ingredient in the dessert tiramisù.

Taleggio A rich, nutty cow's-milk
cheese, from Bergamo

Panettone

Panettone—literally "big bread"—is now popular across Italy and beyond, but
it has its roots in Milan. A popular Christmas food (an estimated 117 million are
baked annually in Italy), it has a distinctive dome shape and uses a light, sweet
dough enriched with butter and eggs and flavored with raisins and candied fruit.
An Easter version is baked in the shape of a dove, or *colomba.*

Factories With a Future

Milan has been adapting buildings for centuries, transforming what were once medieval churches and palaces into galleries, stores, and museums. Today the trend continues, but now the buildings being repurposed are many of the factories abandoned following the decline of the manufacturing industry in the 1970s. Former factory spaces across the city provide often architecturally outstanding homes for galleries and other cultural enterprises.

■ CINEMA AND COMIC

One of the pioneers in the use of Milan's industrial spaces is **Museo Interattivo del Cinema** (Interactive Museum of the Cinema; *Viale Fulvio Testi 121, tel 02 87242114, closed Mon., €€*), which opened in 2001 in a former cigarette factory near the Brera and Garibaldi neighborhoods. Even if you don't speak Italian, its collection of cinema memorabilia is a must for any movie buff. Three years later it was followed by the nearby **Hangar Bicocca** (*Via Chiese 2, tel 02 6611573, hangarbicocca .org, closed Mon.–Wed.*), an area for temporary exhibitions of contemporary art incorporated into the former AnsaldoBreda rolling stock factory. Well out of town is **Wow Spazio Fumetto** (*Viale Campania 12, tel 02 49524744, closed Mon. & Aug.*), devoted to the comic strip, which opened in 2011 in part of the Motta confectionary factory.

■ LAMBRATE

Much of the Milan suburb of Lambrate has been rejuvenated by the conversion of former factories, and it now hums with new stores, bars, B&Bs, restaurants, microbreweries, and more. One example of this transformation is **Faema** on Via Ventura 3–15, now a creative and professional center for some 500 architects, designers, and journalists in a space that once produced coffee machines. Nearer to Parco Sempione, the **Fabbrica del Vapore** (*Via Procaccini 4*) has provided a similar catalyst for change as a cultural and artistic center for youth within a former tramcar and locomotive factory.

Hangar Bicocca exhibits contemporary art in a former railroad factory.

■ THE BIG TWO

Two major projects in the Ticinese and Navigli area exemplify the trend of factory transformation. One, the **Museo delle Culture** (see p. 169; *Via Tortona 56*), is housed in the former home of Ansaldo, once one of Italy's leading engineering firms. The other is the **Fondazione Prada** *(Largo Isarco 2, tel 02 54670515, fondazioneprada.org)*, a gallery and arts center that links striking new buildings with a revamped former state distillery built in 1909. The center hosts temporary exhibitions, a children's area, and part of the permanent art collection accumulated by the Prada fashion house.

■ THE NIGHT SHIFT

Taking on night duties can become a welcome assignment if the factory becomes a luxury hotel. **Magna Pars Suites** *(Via Vincenzo Forcella 6, tel 02 8338371, magnapars-suitesmilano .it)* in the Tortona district once had purpose as a cosmetics factory. Now it offers guests 28 suites overlooking the trees and flowering shrubs of the interior garden. **Hotel nhow** *(Via Tortona 35, tel 02 4898861, nhow-hotels .com)*, located well outside the city center, offers accommodations and an art gallery on the site of the former General Electric factory.

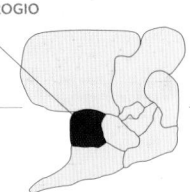

Corso Magenta to Sant'Ambrogio

Art and science are the two themes of this itinerary in the Corso Magenta area. Here Leonardo da Vinci painted "The Last Supper" for his patron, Ludovico il Moro. The most important collection of models of Leonardo's machines can be seen at the Museo della Scienza e della Tecnologia (Museum of Science and Technology), housed in a former Benedictine monastery. Next door, San Vittore al Corpo serves as both a church and a small gallery of fine regional art of the 16th and 17th centuries, as does the nearby Chiesa di San Maurizio. The artistic circle is completed as traces of Leonardo interweave with those of Donato Bramante, the great Renaissance architect, who designed the tribune, the Sacrestia Vecchia, and the cloister of Santa Maria delle Grazie. He also created the two cloisters of the nearby Università Cattolica; these include the ruins of the monastery of the Basilica di Sant'Ambrogio, a masterpiece of Lombard Romanesque.

◀ **The Basilica di
Sant'Ambrogio
centers this artistic
and historic
neighborhood.**

Corso Magenta to Sant'Ambrogio

Ludovico il Moro, Leonardo, and Bramante are three exceptional guides for this itinerary in the area of the Basilica di Sant'Ambrogio.

❷ Civico Museo Archeologico (see p. 132) Within the former Monastero Maggiore, once the most important convent in the city, lies this rich collection of Greek, Etruscan, Roman, and early medieval art. For more treasures, continue straight down the left side of Corso Magenta.

❸ Museo Martinitt e Stelline (see p. 133) A typically Milanese story is told through interactive technology in the what was once the main girls' orphanage of the city. Cross over Corso Magenta to reach Santa Maria delle Grazie.

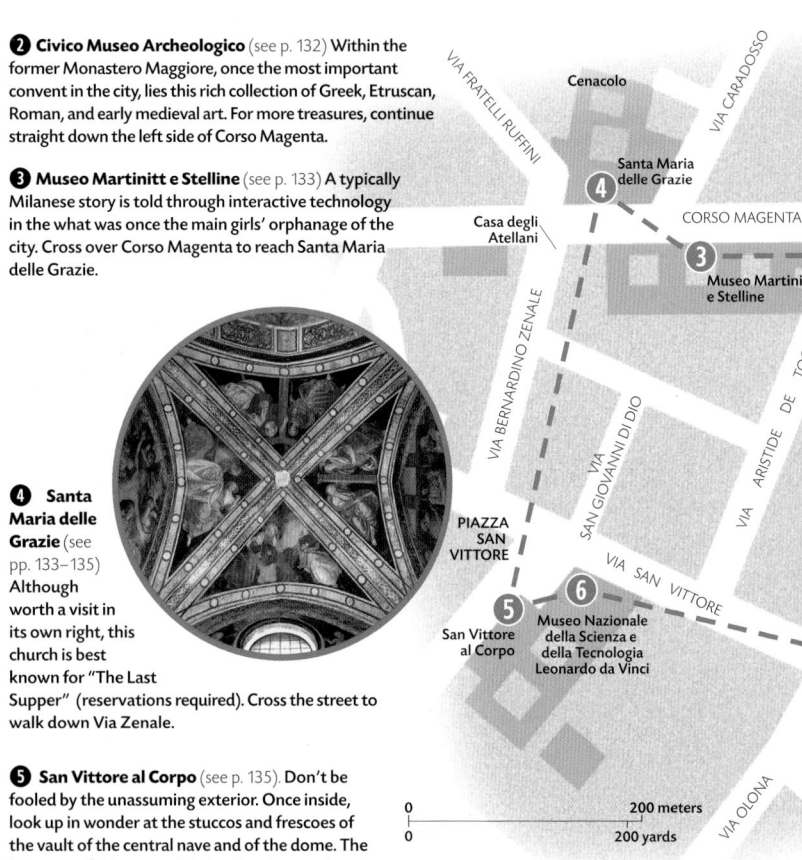

❹ Santa Maria delle Grazie (see pp. 133–135) Although worth a visit in its own right, this church is best known for "The Last Supper" (reservations required). Cross the street to walk down Via Zenale.

❺ San Vittore al Corpo (see p. 135). Don't be fooled by the unassuming exterior. Once inside, look up in wonder at the stuccos and frescoes of the vault of the central nave and of the dome. The Museum of Science and Technology is next door.

Cenacolo

VIA FRATELLI RUFFINI

VIA CARADOSSO

Santa Maria delle Grazie

CORSO MAGENTA

Casa degli Atellani

Museo Martinitt e Stelline

VIA BERNARDINO ZENALE

VIA ARISTIDE DE TOGNI

VIA SAN GIOVANNI DI DIO

PIAZZA SAN VITTORE

VIA SAN VITTORE

San Vittore al Corpo

Museo Nazionale della Scienza e della Tecnologia Leonardo da Vinci

VIA OLONA

0 — 200 meters
0 — 200 yards

**CORSO MAGENTA TO SANT'AMBROGIO   DISTANCE: 0.8 MILE (1.3 KM)
TIME: ABOUT 8 HOURS   METRO START: CAIROLI, LINE 1**

1 San Maurizio al Monastero Maggiore (see p. 132) The richness and quality of this church's frescoes, by masters such as Luini and Peterzano, are comparable to those of the Sistine Chapel in Rome. After admiring them, go to the museum next door.

San Nicolao

Palazzo Litta

LARGO D'ANCONA

CORSO MAGENTA

San Maurizio al Monastero Maggiore

VIA VINCENZO MONTI

VIA E. PANZACCHI

Civico Museo Archeologico

VIA CARDUCCI

VIA SANT'AGNESE

VIA NIRONE

Giardino Aristide Calderini

VIA G. MARRADI

VIA G. MELLERIO

GIOSUE

PIAZZA SANT'AMBROGIO

VIA SANTA VALERIA

LARGO GEMELLI

VIA LUDOVICO NECCHI

PIAZZA SANT'AMBROGIO

7 Sant'Ambrogio (see pp. 138–139) A grand entrance leads into this basilica, founded by St. Ambrose in 379 and heart of Milanese religious life. From here it is a short walk to the Ticinese and Navigli area, great for restaurants and nightlife.

7 Sant'Ambrogio

Università Cattolica

Pusterla di Sant'Ambrogio

6 Museo Nazionale della Scienza e della Tecnologia Leonardo da Vinci (see pp. 136–137) The development of science is illustrated here in the former monastery of the Olivetani. Follow Via San Vittore, then turn left on Via Carducci until you see the church.

Detail of the fresco on the dividing wall of Monastero Maggiore, a work by Bernardino Luini

San Maurizio al Monastero Maggiore

1 Behind the gray facade of the church of San Maurizio, belonging to the **Monastero Maggiore delle Benedettine,** is a blaze of 16th-century frescoes, often compared to the those of the Sistine Chapel. Here, the wall dividing the area for the faithful commoners from the nuns' choir has been decorated by two of the greatest masters of the 16th century, Bernardino Luini and Simone Peterzano. Luini painted the frescoes on the dividing wall and the ones of the **Besozzi Chapel** (the third on the right), with the cycle of St. Catherine. The work of Peterzano, Caravaggio's teacher, can be seen on the inside facade, with the "Return of the Prodigal Son" and the "Casting Out of the Money Changers." Don't miss another of the masterpieces, the beautifully decorated **great organ** by Gian Giacomo Antegnati commissioned in 1554 by the nuns of San Maurizio.

Corso Magenta 13 • Closed Sun.–Mon. • Metro: Cordusio, Cairoli, Line 1; Cadorna, Line 1, 2 • Bus: 18, 50, 57, 58, 61, 94 • Tram: 1, 4, 16, 27

Civico Museo Archeologico

2 Expanded in 2011 at its new location on Via Nirone (containing the early medieval, Etruscan, and Greek exhibits), the Archaeological Museum of Milan is housed in one of the city's most picturesque buildings, the former **convent of the Monastero Maggiore of San Maurizio.** Among the interesting exhibits on display are the **Coppa Trivulzio,** a delicate cage cup dating from the late Roman Empire (third to fourth century), the **Patera of Parabiago,** a ritual silver dish of the mid-fourth century, and treasures from excavations of Caesarea Maritima, the city founded by Herod the Great in honor of Augustus.

Corso Magenta 15 • tel 02 88445208 • Closed Mon. • € • Metro: Cordusio, Cairoli, Line 1; Cadorna, Line 1, 2 • Bus: 18, 50, 57, 58, 61, 94 • Tram: 1, 4, 16, 27

Museo Martinitt e Stelline

③ The Martinitt and Stelline Museum opened in the right wing of the former Stelline orphanage in 2009, offering a different view of the city's past. It is devoted to telling the story of two of the most important Milanese institutions committed to helping orphans. Multimedia displays outline the lives of the resident girls (the Stelline), and the boys (the Martinitt), in the 19th and 20th centuries, giving a real sense of their time in this building. Be sure to visit the classroom faithfully reconstructed as if the fourth class of Martinitt were being taught here in the 1872–1873 school year. Today the visiting public can choose the subjects of the lessons on an interactive screen, sit at the school desks, and interact with a virtual teacher. Instructional for all ages, this will be a particularly intriguing stop for children and a welcome break from the fabulous artwork on display elsewhere.

SAVVY **TRAVELER**

Among the stately buildings of Corso Magenta there is a hidden park that few people know—a secret garden *(entry through Via Terraggio no. 5)*. A gift to Lorenzo de' Medici from Galeazzo Visconti and Ludovico il Moro, the garden was closed for 70 years but reopened to the public in 2010.

Corso Magenta 57 • tel 02 43006522 • Closed Sun.–Mon. • Metro: Cadorna, Line 1, 2; Conciliazione, Line 1 • Bus: 18, 50, 58, 94 • Tram: 16, 19

Santa Maria delle Grazie

④ The church of Santa Maria delle Grazie is best known for **"Cenacolo"** ("The Last Supper"), painted by Leonardo da Vinci in its adjoining monastery (see pp. 140–141). Most people come here to see the painting, but if you have time, or have been unable to get a ticket for entry (see pp. 134–135), then the church is worth a visit in its own right. It was begun in 1465 and completed in the 1480s, but—under orders of Ludovico il Moro—the church was almost immediately transformed by the architect Donato Bramante into a more Renaissance-styled mausoleum for the Sforza family. Among the changes he made, Bramante constructed the massive apses above which rises the church's drum-shaped dome, with circular motifs everywhere. He also designed the sacristy, the choir, and the wonderful "cloister of frogs," so named for the statues that adorn the fountain in the center of the beautifully proportioned garden.

Entry to the church of Santa Maria is free and straightforward, unlike viewing "The Last Supper," where the precarious condition of the painting imposes strict limits on visitors: Only 30 people at a time can enter for a maximum of 15 minutes. Booking entry is compulsory and generally tickets are reserved two to three months in advance. Tickets for future months become available on set days, which are listed on the official ticketing site, *vivaticket.it.* Be sure to buy them as soon as they go on sale, as they're often snapped up very quickly by travel agents.

Alternatively, you can arrive at the ticket office at the opening time of 8 a.m. on the day you want to visit and ask if any slots are available from canceled agency reservations (called *prenotazioni annullate*). Booking a tour with an agency guarantees entry along with a guide but may cost €50 or more. Most will agree it is worth the effort to study Jesus' mysterious expression, halfway between sadness and

To protect the treasured painting, visitation is limited to small groups, with 15 minutes to vie **Leonardo's masterpiece in the refectory.**

contemplation, which has baffled critics and historians for centuries.

Piazza Santa Maria delle Grazie 2 • "The Last Supper" online booking: vivaticket.it • Reservations tel 02 92800360, lines open Mon.–Sat. 8 a.m.–6:30 p.m. • Church closed daily noon– 3:30 p.m., "The Last Supper" closed Mon. • "The Last Supper" €€, reservations required • Metro: Conciliazione, Line 1 • Bus: 50, 58 • Tram: 1, 16, 27

San Vittore al Corpo

⑤ After experiencing the crowds at "The Last Supper," a visit to this stunning and underrated church provides a break and the chance to absorb beauty in peace. Do not be fooled by the unassuming exterior, as within you will be greeted by soaring columns and a sumptuous interior covered with fine works of sacred art.

The central nave of San Vittore al Corpo with its frescoed barrel vault, the work of Procaccini

The church itself rose up in an imperial and early Christian burial ground, around the fourth-century Roman mausoleum of Emperor Valentinian II, who died in 392. (Portions of this area remain beneath the adjacent convent, now the Museum of Science and Technology.) It was rebuilt in the 11th and 12th centuries, but today the church has been restored to its 16th-century magnificence, doubling as a museum of the art of the 16th and 17th centuries. Lavish, colorful painting edged in gold is seemingly everywhere; the dome has wonderful frescoes by Daniele Crespi and Guglielmo Caccia Moncalvo, while the barrel vault above the central nave is decorated with frescoes by Ercole Procaccini, who, with his brother Camillo, worked in the church for many years. Camillo's hand can be seen in his depiction of the "Life of St. Gregory" filling the right-hand apse. Scenes of the life of St. Benedict are carved into the elaborate wooden choir stalls. Of particular note is the chapel of Sant'Antonio Abate, covered with frescoes created by Crespi in 1619.

Via San Vittore 25 • tel 02 48005351 • www.basilicasanvittore.it • Closed July–Aug. • Metro: Sant'Ambrogio, Line 2 • Bus: 50, 58, 94

Enrico Toti, the first submarine built in Italy after World War II and launched in 1967, "beached" at the Museum of Science and Technology in 2005. The guided tour inside the submarine, popular with all ages, is by reservation only.

Tel 02 48555330, museoscienza.org, €€

Museo Nazionale della Scienza e della Tecnologia Leonardo da Vinci

6 In the museum's vast 27,000 square feet (25,000 sq m) of exhibition space you can follow the history of science, technology, and industry up to the present. You can easily spend hours, or even days here. Luckily, the museum's immense stock of objects (15,000 technical, scientific, and artistic items) is organized by departments so you can focus on what interests you the most: Materials, Transport, Energy, Communication, Space, the **Leonardo da Vinci Art & Science Collection,** New Frontiers, or Science for Children. But no matter what your passion, be sure to wander the first-floor (one flight up)

Young minds creating at the Museum of Science and Technology

exhibits devoted to Leonardo da Vinci, with fascinating modern models based on the genius's sketches, among other things. Most people think of Leonardo as a painter, but he was also a talented musician, engineer, sculptor, and an astute observer of the world around him. His studies of human anatomy and expression, nature, and how things work led to his many innovative ideas.

Another can't-miss area is the impressive ground-floor section devoted to means of transportation—covering road, sea, rail, and air. The **air and sea section** alone displays 11 aircraft, including the first Italian fighter, the Macchi Nieuport Ni10 (1915). In the **rail transportation section** is a horse-drawn tram (1885), and the locomotive Gr 552, shown at the Paris Universal Exposition of 1889. The water transportation section showcases the **brigantine schooner** *Ebe* (1921) as well as a rich collection of figureheads. The museum's flagship, and a particular favorite of families, is the **submarine** *Enrico Toti* (see p. 31). Note that the popular guided tours of this intriguing vessel require a separate ticket, booked in advance (see sidebar opposite), or by purchase from the museum reception area on the day of your visit.

Via San Vittore 21 • tel 02 485551 • museoscienza.org • Closed Mon. • €€€ • Metro: Sant'Ambrogio, Line 2 • Bus: 50, 58, 94

Sant'Ambrogio

 See pp. 138–139.

Piazza Sant'Ambrogio 15 • tel 02 86450895 • Metro: Sant'Ambrogio, Line 2 • Bus: 50, 58, 94

GOOD **EATS**

■ LA BRISA
Traditional dishes revisited and made lighter, but still focused on flavor: This is the hallmark of the cuisine of Antonio Facciolo, who for some years has been in charge of this celebrated restaurant with a garden situated behind Corso Magenta. **Via Brisa 15, tel 02 86450521, €€€€**

■ MARTA
Pane e Acqua, the restaurant of Rossana Orlandi, has changed its chef and its name. The kitchen is now associated with Marta Pulini, chef of Francescetta 8, bistro of Massimo Bottura's starred Osteria Francescana. **Via Matteo Bandello 14, tel 02 48198622, closed Sun., €€€€€**

■ OM FOOD
There are two reasons for stopping at OM Food (open from breakfast to *aperitivo* time). The first is the strictly organic food, the second is the perfect context: a charming octagonal courtyard inside an aristocratic palazzo in Corso Magenta. **Corso Magenta 12, tel 02 36522069, €€**

Sant'Ambrogio

Established in the fourth century by the patron saint of Milan, this basilica, together with the Duomo, is the city's spiritual heart.

The gabled facade of Sant'Ambrogio is approached through a series of elegant porticos.

Founded by the popular St. Ambrose between 379 and 386 as the Basilica Martyrum (Martyrs' Basilica), the church was built in an area reserved for the burial of martyrs. A born leader, Ambrose convinced Augustine, a pagan, to turn to Christianity. Since the ninth century, the building has undergone a number of modifications; its current status as a masterpiece of Lombard Romanesque architecture dates from work carried out between 1088 and 1099.

■ STILICHO'S SARCOPHAGUS

There are very few memorials in the church of St. Ambrose. The most famous is the early Christian sarcophagus of Stilicho (fourth century), on the left side of the central nave, hidden between the columns of the medieval pulpit. Decorated on all four sides, the imposing Carrara marble sarcophagus was long thought to contain the remains of the general Stilicho and his wife Serena, daughter of the Emperor Honorius, a legend now disproven.

■ SACELLO DI SAN VITTORE IN CIEL D'ORO

To have a close encounter with St. Ambrose himself, visit the poetically named Sacello di San Vittore in Ciel d'Oro (Oratory of San Vittore in a Golden Sky), to the right of the main altar. This chapel was built in the fourth century by Maternus, bishop of Milan, to preserve the remains of the martyr Vittorius, whose likeness gazes down from the glowing gold mosaic in the center of the dome. Look along the side wall of the apse for the oldest and most realistic depiction of St. Ambrose, portrayed in a mosaic between Sts. Gervasius and Protasio.

■ THE ALTAR OF VOLVINIUS

At the heart of the church, protected by the four red columns of the richly decorated ciborium, shines the golden altar of Volvinius (mid-ninth century). It takes its name from the talented goldsmith who built this masterpiece in 835. The front of the altar has embossed gold cover plates showing stories from the life of Jesus; embossed silver plates at the back of the altar illustrate the life of St. Ambrose.

■ THE CRYPT

Descend to the crypt, built when the basilica was modified in the middle of the tenth century. Since 1874 this great underground space has been preserved behind glass, through which the skeletal remains of Sts. Ambrose, Gervasius, and Protasio can be seen, moved here from beneath the golden altar.

Piazza Sant'Ambrogio 15 • tel 02 86450895 • Metro: Sant'Ambrogio, Line 2 • Bus: 50, 58, 94

"The Last Supper"

No other work of art is as associated with Milan as "The Last Supper"—"L'Ultima Cena" or "Cenacolo" in Italian—one of the most famous paintings in the world. This damaged but dazzling masterpiece by Leonardo da Vinci will be high on the list of priorities for most visitors, but its popularity and precarious state mean that you have to plan and book well in advance to join the limited number of people allowed to see the masterpiece (see p. 134).

Leonardo da Vinci painted his masterpiece for the monks of Santa Maria delle Grazie (above). Opposite: Detail from "The Last Supper," much restored from Leonardo's fragile original.

The Refectory

The painting survives in the space for which it was originally created, the refectory of the Dominican monastery attached to Santa Maria delle Grazie. This was where the monks gathered to eat, making the Last Supper an obvious choice of subject for its decoration. Leonardo painted the fresco between 1494 and 1497 and in it captures the dramatic moment after Christ has announced to his disciples that one of them will betray him. Around the figure of Jesus, the artist arranged the apostles in four groups of three, painting their emotional reactions to the revelation of Jesus with consummate skill. Doubting Thomas can be recognized by his raised finger, Philip by his folded arms and fearful expression, worried that he may be the betrayer. Peter is partly obscured by the figure of Judas, who hurries forward with his 30 pieces of silver. Leonardo is said to have spent months scouring the streets and prisons of Milan searching for a sufficiently evil-looking model to represent Judas.

Oil and Water

For all the fame of "The Last Supper," it can be a shock to see the painting's faded appearance. This is primarily due to Leonardo's determination to use oil paints and tempera (pigment fixed with egg yolk) instead of the traditional techniques of fresco. Painted onto wet, or fresh (fresco) plaster, pigments in water bind powerfully to a porous wall in a strong chemical reaction as the plaster dries. Painted as oil, they sit on the surface and quickly lift off in the face of damp and weathering. Oil, however, allows far greater choice of color and tone, and in the short term produces more subtle and striking murals. In the long term, as here, however, most such paintings suffer marked deterioration. Poor early restorations as well as other damage further altered the original.

CHURCH **TREASURES**

The refectory of Santa Maria delle Grazie is not the only sacred space in Milan to contain masterful paintings. Others include:

San Fedele (see p. 60) This church shelters the emotional "Deposition of Christ" by Simone Peterzano (who taught Caravaggio), along with other artwork moved from Santa Maria alla Scala when it was demolished to make way for the famous theater.

Santa Maria della Passione (see p. 75) Another view of the "Last Supper," here by Gaudenzio Ferrari

Santa Maria presso San Satiro (see p. 117) This small sanctuary is notable for Donato Bramante's triumph in trompe l'oeil behind the altar and in a false choir.

Sweet Shops

In a city that even dedicated an expo to food and flavors (in 2015), there are many temptations, especially when it comes to dessert. Milan knows how to deliver delicious treats that go far beyond the traditional panettone.

■ SWEET SHOPPING CENTER

Hidden behind a door near Corso Magenta, in a little building set in a quiet courtyard, delicous tarts, mousse, and other sweets inspired by the great French tradition await at **I Dolci di Galdina** (*Via Terraggio 9, tel 02 89073280, closed Sun.*). The great traditional Milanese classics can be found in abundance at nearby **Marchesi** (*Via Santa Maria alla Porta 11, tel 02 862770, closed Mon.*), known for its imaginative window displays. Another excellent choice is **Cova** (*Via Montenapoleone 8, tel 02 76005599*), founded in 1817, in the heart of the Fashion District.

Three sweet stops near the Giardini Pubblici include **Pavé** (*Via Felice Casati 27, tel 02 94392259, closed Mon.*), where customers are welcomed by comfortable furniture and the perfect lighting for reading, as well as excellent brioches and imaginative cakes of fine pastry. A more traditional atmosphere awaits at **Sissi** (*Piazza Risorgimento 6, tel 02 76014664, closed Tues.*), a popular pastry shop with a small garden perfect for summer breakfasts of freshly baked pastries and quiche. Close by is the equally friendly **Marotin** (*Via Archimede 59, tel 02 73957790, closed Sun.*), a French café with small tables, iron chairs, and a counter full of cakes and tempting pastries.

■ BEYOND THE CENTER

Chocolate is the top product of one of the most acclaimed pastry chefs in Milan, the German **Ernst Knam** (*Via Anfossi 10, tel 02 55194448, eknam.com*), a master at combining unexpected flavors such as a chocolate tart with pumpkin, pistachios, and Maldon salt, or a mousse of eggplant and chocolate. You will find him in southeast Milan, along with the glamorous pastry shop **Giacomo** (*Via Pasquale Sottocorno 5, tel 02 76319147, giacomopasticceria.com, closed Sun.*). Visit not only for the tasty specialties but also for the setting, with antique furniture and a 19th-century floral ceiling evoking

Gelato comes in many flavors, sure to delight.

a bygone time. Try the *bomba*, a pastry stuffed with mascarpone cream and wild strawberries. Another shop with deep roots is **Le Dolci Tradizioni** *(Via Ampére 122, tel 02 2820612)*, in the Città Studi area, known for its chocolate cake with fresh raspberries, tarte tatin, and pear-and-chocolate tart.

■ GELATO OR ICE CREAM?

In Italy, there's no distinction between ice cream and gelato; everything is called gelato, and ice cream is seen as the English translation of the word. The best? Since 1959 it has been a scoop from **Gelateria Umberto** *(Piazza Cinque Giornate 4, tel 02 5458113)*, a reliable destination in southeast Milan for those who love classic flavors. While in this neighborhood, stop by the also excellent **Giova** *(Corso Indipendenza 20, tel 02 712657)*, where you can enjoy the Langhe hazelnut, Bronte pistachio, and Amalfi lemon flavors. Chocolate lovers strolling near the Galleria may prefer the more fashionable **Cioccolati Italiani** *(Via San Raffaele 6, tel 02 89093820)*, which offers hot chocolate sauce. Finally, **Gelato Giusto** *(Via San Gregorio 17, tel 02 29510284, closed Mon.)* excels in its ingredients and creative combinations.

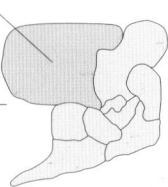

Around Parco Sempione

Like other parts of the city, the area around Parco Sempione has undergone many changes between the 19th and 20th centuries. Castello Sforzesco, residence of the Sforza family, was redesigned and rebuilt at the end of the 19th century to hold museums and libraries. Napoleon chose this part of Milan as its civic center, arranging the construction of an arena, a triumphal arch, and the unfinished ring of the Foro Buonaparte. Today these monuments share the setting with others built in the revitalized Parco Sempione, itself a former ducal garden and parade ground. These include the aquarium, an art nouveau masterpiece built for Expo 1906; the Palazzo dell'Arte, built in 1933 for the Triennale exhibition of decorative arts and now an excellent display area for traveling art exhibitions; and the Design Museum.

◄ **The fountain-filled plaza fronting the landmark Castello Sforzesco marks the center of a tourist-friendly pedestrian zone.**

Around Parco Sempione

Fill your day exploring a royal palace, a vast green space, and landmarks in modern design, ending in a prime nightlife area dominated by a Napoleonic arch.

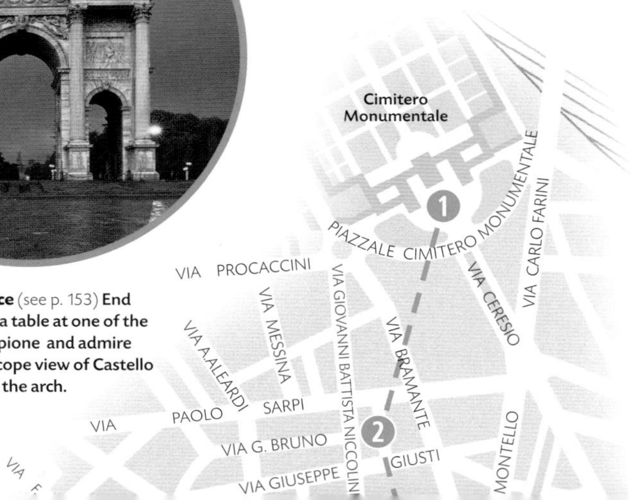

0   200 meters
0   200 yards

Cimitero Monumentale

❶ **Cimitero Monumentale** (see p. 148) **Start your walk at this incredible open-air sculpture museum within the cemetery built by Maciachini after the unification of Italy. Then go down Via Procaccini and turn left down Via Messina, until you get to pedestrian Via Paolo Sarpi.**

❷ **Chinatown** (see p. 148) Ready for lunch? Enjoy Chinatown, an area centered on Via Paolo Sarpi recently pedestrianized and lined with Chinese bars and restaurants. From here, follow Via Rosmini and Via Canonica until you see the park.

❾ **Arco della Pace** (see p. 153) End your day sitting at a table at one of the bars in Piazza Sempione and admire the so-called telescope view of Castello Sforzesco through the arch.

PIAZZALE CIMITERO MONUMENTALE

VIA PROCACCINI

VIA A. ALEARDI

VIA MESSINA

VIA GIOVANNI BATTISTA NICCOLINI

VIA CERESIO

VIA CARLO FARINI

VIA BRAMANTE

PAOLO   SARPI

VIA

VIA G. BRUNO

VIA GIUSEPPE

GIUSTI

MONTELLO

3 Acquario Civico (see p. 149)
Explore the third oldest aquarium in Europe, created for the 1906 International Exposition. Exit on Viale Gadio, cut across the park, and bear right until you see the arena.,

4 Arena Civica "Gianni Brera" (see p. 150) The amphitheater commissioned by Napoleon is still an excellent sports facility. Turn left as you exit the arena and cut across the park to the Castello Sforzesco.

5 Castello Sforzesco (see pp. 154–155) Once one of the most sumptuous courts of the Renaissance, today this is an unequaled center of culture and museums in the city. When you are finished, reenter the park.

6 Parco Sempione (see pp. 150–151) Stretch your legs or enjoy a picnic in this large city park running from Passo del Sempione toward the Duomo. To reach the Triennale, cross the park bearing left, with your back to the castle.

7 Triennale (see p. 151–152) A short walk in the green of the park will take you into the future at this temple of design and architecture. The Torre Branca is steps away.

8 Torre Branca (see pp. 152–153) Enjoy the view over Milan and its surroundings from the top of this tower. Then head for the big arch at the far end of the park and Corso Sempione, a popular nightlife area.

AROUND PARCO SEMPIONE DISTANCE: 2.7 MILES (4.4 KM)
TIME: ABOUT 5 HOURS METRO START: GARIBALDI, LINE 2, 5

AROUND PARCO SEMPIONE

CORSO GARIBALDI
VIA
PIAZZA LEGA LOMBARDA
VIA LEGNANO
Acquario Civico
FORO BUONAPARTE
VIA TIVOLI
PIAZZA CASTELLO
Arena Civica
VIA ELVEZIA
VIA A. BERTARELLI
VIALE
MALTA
Castello Sforzesco
Parco Sempione
Triennale
VIALE EMILIO ALEMAGNA
VIALE MOLIERE
VIA G. LEOPARDI
VIA L. CANONICA
V. ALFIERI
Arco della Pace
VIA A. SAN GIORGIO
Torre Branca
VIA MARIO PAGANO
VIA G. REVERE
CORSO SEMPIONE
VIA CANOVA
VIA MELZI D'ERIL
LONDONIO

Cimitero Monumentale

1 For the Milanese, the Cimitero Monumentale is *the* cemetery. Being buried in this graveyard—designed by Carlo Maciachini and inaugurated at the end of 1866—is almost a status symbol. For the living, wandering through the beautiful grounds offers a chance to celebrate the dead and enjoy the elaborate shrines and monuments commissioned by the great families of Milan. Men of learning, civil society, and industry have left here not only their remains but signs of their existence through the numerous works of art scattered all over what is really a marvelous open-air museum. All the outstanding architects and sculptors of the 19th and 20th centuries have left their mark here, from Luca Beltrami to Lucio Fontana, from Arturo Martini to Giò Pomodoro, from Adolfo Wildt to Enrico Butti. The main memorial chapel, the **Famedio,** opened in 1833, is the pantheon of famous Milanese. In this neo-medieval building Alessandro Manzoni, Arturo Toscanini, Salvatore Quasimodo, Anna Kuliscioff, and Eugenio Montale are commemorated, as well as many others.

Piazzale Cimitero Monumentale • tel 02 88465600 • Closed Mon. • Metro: Garibaldi F. S., Line 2, 5 • Bus: 37, 70, 94 • Tram: 2,4, 7

Chinatown

2 The district between Via Canonica and Via Paolo Sarpi enfolds the oldest Chinatown in Italy. The neighborhood here developed in the 1920s, when the main business was the silk-tie trade. Since the mid-1990s the Chinese population in the area has increased and commercial operations have multiplied. The chief activity now is selling clothes and leather goods. Via Paolo Sarpi, recently pedestrianized, is lined with Chinese bars and restaurants, fashion wholesalers, and even a tofu shop and a bubble-tea bar. It's a great place for a Chinese meal; **Jubin** *(Via Paolo Sarpi 1)* and **China Long** *(Via Paolo Sarpi 42)* are reliable choices.

Via Paolo Sarpi & Via Canonica • Metro: Moscova, Line 2 • Bus: 94 • Tram: 2, 4, 12, 14

Acquario Civico

3 There may not be tanks populated by sharks and dolphins in the Civic Aquarium, but you will learn a lot about what more commonly surrounds you: mountain streams with trout, rivers with carp, and the Italian and Mediterranean marine environment. Note the enormous statue of Neptune by the entrance, as well as the creatures of the deep (in concrete) studding the exterior. Inside, the exhibits have recently been rethought for an enhanced experience. This art nouveau gem, designed in the Liberty style by Sebastiano Locati, is the only building that remains from the original 225 structures constructed for the International Exposition of 1906, organized in Milan to celebrate the opening of the Simplon Tunnel connecting Italy with Switzerland. It sits on the edge of the Parco Sempione, with an entrance on Viale Gadio.

Viale Gadio 2 • tel 02 88445392 • acquariocivicomilano.eu • Closed Mon. • € • Metro: Lanza, Line 2 • Bus: 45, 57, 61 • Tram: 3, 4, 7, 12, 14

The Mediterranean fish tank bridge of the Acquario Civico, itself an art nouveau masterpiece

Arena Civica "Gianni Brera"

4 The elegant Arena Civica, right next to Parco Sempione, was designed by the neoclassical architect Luigi Canonica, who was inspired by the Circus Maximus in Rome. It was opened by Napoleon himself in 1807. Since then the arena has hosted naval battle reenactments, Buffalo Bill's Wild West Show, and soccer and rugby matches; 12 athletic world records have been set here. With a capacity of up to 10,000 spectators, today it continues to host sport events and rock concerts, and it remains the most important athletics facility in Milan. It was recently renamed in honor of the sportswriter and journalist Gianni Brera. Thanks to the FAI (Italian Environmental Fund), which now manages the area, **Palazzina Appiani,** the 19th-century building at the entrance of the amphitheater, is open to the public for special exhibits and events. Its fine rooms include the **Sala del Pulvinare** overlooking the park and decorated with a frieze by Andrea Appiani.

Largo Byron 2 • tel 02 88448360 • Metro: Lanza, Moscova, Line 2 • Bus: 57, 70, 94 • Tram: 3, 4, 12, 14 . 43

Castello Sforzesco

5 See pp. 154–155.

Piazza Castello–Piazza d'Armi • tel 02 88463700 • milanocastello.it • Museums closed Mon. • Museums € • Metro: Cadorna, Cairoli, Line 1; Cadorna, Lanza, Line 2 • Bus: 18, 50, 57, 58, 61, 94 • Tram: 1, 2, 4, 12, 14, 19

Parco Sempione

6 The restoration of Parco Sempione (Sempione Park) was completed in 2003, returning to the city a green oasis enjoyed by all. The enclosed area has almost doubled, making it even more of a paradise for children as well as adults, including runners who enjoy a 2-mile (3.2 km) circuit of marked paths. In addition to providing a welcome way to enjoy the outdoors, the park touches upon several of the city's most important buildings, the Arco della Pace, the Castello Sforzesco, the Triennale, the Civic Arena, and the aquarium among them. The city's second park, it was designed by Emilio Alemagna in the English-garden style in 1890 on the former Piazza d'Armi. Look within the gardens for several important works of art, including the **"Mysterious Baths Fountain,"** one of Giorgio De Chirico's last works, in the gardens of the Triennale. Interesting buildings also dot its landscape, such as the steel-and-concrete **Biblioteca del Parco** (Library of the Park) built in the Monte Tordo area for the 1954 Triennale by Ico Parisi and Silvio Longhi. Look inside the library for majolica decoration by Bruno Munari, while outside there is a statue by Francesco Somaini and a bas-relief by Mauro Reggiani.

Metro: Cadorna, Cairoli, Line 1; Cadorna, Lanza, Line 2 • Bus: 43, 57, 61, 70, 94 • Tram: 1, 2, 4, 12, 19, 27

Triennale

7 The Triennale of Milan is the ultimate aesthetic experience, starting with its host building, the **Palazzo dell'Arte.** Designed by Giovanni Muzio in the rationalist style, it opened on the Parco Sempione in 1933 as a vast space for Milan's huge decorative arts exhibition, held every three years (a *triennale*). But even on off years you can enter the building to enjoy intriguing displays featuring the permanent collection, as well as many temporary exhibits, all focusing on how visual and decorative arts, design, fashion, and audiovisual production meet in a continuous interplay of new trends.

In 2007 the **Triennale Design Museum** opened here to give visitors the opportunity to find out about the excellence of Italian design through "interpretations" that vary year to year. Drawing on its rich collection, the museum presents an ever changing exhibition of themes and subjects that are constantly renewed, to give

Designed by Giovanni Muzio, the Palazzo dell'Arte has hosted the Triennale since 1933, and includes a museum of architecture and design.

GOOD **EATS**

■ CERESIO7
It's like being in New York, but you are at Porta Volta, where Dean and Dan Caten, owners of Dsquared^2, opened a rooftop restaurant with swimming pools in the historic Palazzo dell'Enel. The dishes are eclectic and the decor is a successful mix of vintage and contemporary design. **Via Ceresio 7, tel 02 31039221, €€€€**

■ L'ESSENZIALE
Run by young chef Gabriele Baldini, this new restaurant offers a modern spin on traditional Italian favorites. Dishes include tartare three ways, and purple risotto with beetroot, foie gras, and gorgonzola **Via Maggi 6, tel 02 45499964, closed Sun., €€€€**

■ UNICO
Enjoy a spectacular view and an open kitchen at chef Fabio Baldassarre's restaurant on the 20th floor of the WJC skyscraper in Portello. Here are creative dishes with seasonal ingredients. **Via Achille Papa 30, tel 02 39261025, €€€€€**

repeat visitors various points of view. The permanent collection of the museum, which includes drawings by Alessandro Mendini, a collection of studio models made by Giovanni Sacchi, and Alessandro Pedretti's collection, is combined and refreshed with the active collaboration of private collections, company museum holdings, specialist collections, and small thematic museums.

If you're ready for a snack after all this art, head over to the on-site **Design Café,** where you can test out an eclectic mix of designer chairs as you enjoy your coffee, gazing through large windows overlooking the park. An outdoor restaurant has recently been added to the panoramic courtyard. Both eateries offer you views of the park, where more than a hundred design works are shown in rotation.

Viale Alemagna 6 • tel 02 724341 • triennale.it • Closed Mon. • €€ • Metro: Cadorna, Line 1, 2 • Bus: 61

Torre Branca

8 Milan's minimalist version of the Eiffel Tower, Torre Branca is celebrated by visitors mainly for the view it offers from its top. Originally opened for the fifth Triennale in 1933, this tubular steel structure designed by Gio Ponti was named Torre Littoria, but for most Milanese it was simply the Torre del Parco (Tower in the Park). In 1997 it became the Torre Branca in recognition of the distillery that financed its restoration, work that included adding a glass-walled elevator. Today it takes just 99 seconds for that elevator to ascend the 350 feet (106.8 m) to the top of the tower. From the viewing platform you can enjoy a breathtaking, 360-degree view of all of Milan. If the weather is cooperating, you can see all the way to the Alps as well as across the Lombardy plain.

Viale Alemagna 6 • tel 02 3314120 • €€ • Metro: Cadorna, Cairoli, Line 1; Cadorna, Lanza, Line 2 • Bus: 18, 50, 57, 58, 61, 94 • Tram: 1, 2, 4, 12, 14, 19

Arco della Pace

9 Dominating the huge Piazza Sempione and facing the Castello Sforzesco, this great neoclassical triple arch was started by Luigi Cagnola in 1807, after Napoleon had given Milan 200,000 francs to commemorate the Battle of Jena (October 1806). Work was interrupted in 1814 and later resumed under the Austrian Emperor Francis I. The Arco della Vittoria (Arch of Victory) then became the Arco della Pace (Arch of Peace), and it was finished after 1838. The arch is made of Baveno granite and clad in Crevola d'Ossola marble. Crane your neck and look to the top to see the bronze chariot pulled by six horses, crowned by a statue of Minerva of Peace flanked by four Victories on horseback. (To give you some idea of the size, Minerva alone is 13 feet, or 4 meters, tall.)

From here, end your day enjoying the many clubs and fashionable restaurants of the area. In this popular district, follow those in the know to enjoy an *aperitivo* along with exploiting some of the well-known gargantuan food buffets. Steps from the arch, **Bhangrabar** *(Corso Sempione 1, tel 02 34934469)* is one of the best happy hour choices in town, with delicious food and excellent cocktails. Typically open from 6 p.m. until 2 a.m., **Wish** *(Corso Sempione 5, tel 02 33103709)*, **Jazz Café** *(Corso Sempione 8, tel 02 33604039)*, and **Kitsch Bar** *(Corso Sempione 5, tel 02 33103788)*, all within the same block, are other popular choices for a night out, especially in summer when the crowd spills onto the square around the Arco.

Piazza Sempione • Metro: Cadorna, Line 1, 2 • Tram: 1

Castello Sforzesco

After a long and varied history, the immense Castello Sforzesco, one of Milan's most imposing landmarks, is now home to several key museums.

Suits of armor on the ground floor of the Corte Ducale within the Castello Sforzesco

Milan's ruling Visconti family began the castle and made it their home in 1368. After 1450 the Sforza family seized power and remodeled the fortress as a residence and seat of one of Europe's leading Renaissance courts. The castle was never quite the same after Milan's defeat by France in 1499, and was alternately remodeled or neglected under French and Austrian occupation across the succeeding centuries. Restoration and rebuilding began in earnest after 1893, and in 1904 much of the complex was reopened as a home for a library, archive, and a collection of museums.

■ MUSEO D'ARTE ANTICA

The first of the Castello Sforzesco's key museums is located in several grand, frescoed rooms around the main **Corte Ducale** (Ducal Courtyard) on the right after you enter the complex. Room 8, the **Sale delle Asse,** is celebrated for a series of botanical frescoes (1498) attributed to Leonardo da Vinci, while other rooms are devoted largely to sculptural work from the 4th to the 18th centuries.

■ THE PINACOTECA

The marvelous *pinacoteca* possesses more than 1,500 fine works of art, of which some 230 are on display at any one time. Many belong to the Lombard and Milanese schools of painting, but acquisitions over the centuries have resulted in a collection of masterpieces from across Italy and beyond. Highlights include "St. Benedict" (1470) by Sicilian painter Antonello da Messina, and Andrea Mantegna's sumptuous "Madonna and Saints With Angels" (1497). Venice, the Marche, and Tuscany are also well represented, with works by Canaletto and Giovanni Bellini, Carlo Crivelli, and Filippo Lippi.

SAVVY **TRAVELER**

The trenches of the battlements and the covered Strada della Ghirlanda that linked the castle to other important buildings in the city are two secret places that you can only visit on a guided tour. Information and bookings are through Ad Artem *(tel 02 6596937, adartem.it),* which also organizes outings to other key sights in the city.

■ PIETÀ RONDANINI

Other museums within the Castello Sforzesco are devoted to musical instruments, the applied arts (including valuable tapestries), and Egyptian mummies, among other things. But the castle's single most famous work of art is Michelangelo's beautiful **Pietà Rondanini,** the last of four versions he created on this theme of the Madonna mourning the crucified Christ. The sculptor was working on the piece at his death in 1564. (Michelangelo himself never set foot in Milan.) It takes its name from the last owners, the Rome-based Rondanini family from whom it was bought by the City of Milan in 1952. The statue, considered a must-see, is housed in the former **Ospedale Spagnolo** (Spanish Hospital), within the castle's western walls.

Piazza Castello–Piazza d'Armi • tel 02 88463700 • milanocastello.it • Museums closed Mon. • Museums € • Metro: Cadorna, Cairoli, Line 1; Cadorna, Lanza, Line 2 • Bus: 18, 50, 57, 58, 61, 94 • Tram: 1, 2, 4, 12, 14, 19

AROUND PARCO SEMPIONE

The City of Leonardo

Leonardo da Vinci arrived in Milan in 1482 as the ambassador of Lorenzo the Magnificent to the court of Ludovico il Moro. The great genius of the Renaissance, then 30 years old, was already a well-known artist in Florence. In ducal Milan, at that time a city of more than 100,000 inhabitants that was open to new technologies, he worked and experimented in engineering, military machines, architecture, and—in his final years here—painting and sculpture. He left the city in 1499, when the arrival of the French army was imminent.

Evidence of a brilliant mind: a study for the head of St. James the Great, with a sketch of what may be the Castello Sforzesco (above). Opposite, a sheet of the Codex Atlanticus illustrating the operation of the city's Navigli, or canals.

A Genius at the Castello

Leonardo da Vinci's most important work at **Castello Sforzesco** is the huge trompe l'oeil painted by the artist in 1498 on the vault of the **Sala delle Asse** (Room of the Wooden Boards). It portrays an incredible arbor made of interwoven mulberry branches supported by strong tree trunks. This hall, where the powerful Sforza family welcomed their guests, is today part of the **Museo d'Arte Antica** (Museum of Ancient Art; see p. 155). Recent restoration revealed the remnants of Leonardo's preparatory drawing under various layers of paint. Since 1935 another key work by Leonardo has been preserved in the castle: the **Trivulzian Codex,** a fascinating "sketchbook" of the artist's time in Milan containing studies of physiognomy, architectural sketches of the Duomo, and plans of war machines and mechanical tools.

Studies of the Navigli

The studies and drawings in the **Codex Atlanticus** (see p. 123) are evidence of Leonardo's interest in the Navigli, the oldest artificial canals in Europe. The Renaissance genius was one of the many engineers who sought to increase the number of waterways to the city, both to supply the necessary water and to create main routes for transporting goods and supplies. Most important, Leonardo built the **Porte Vinciane per la Martesana,** the waterway between Trezzo sull'Adda and Milan linking the Adda and Ticino Rivers. Then the locks made for the **Conca dell'Incoronata** were repeated along all the Navigli and later spread all over Europe.

COMPLETE **LEONARDO**

The Ambrosiana (see pp. 122–123) Leonardo's Codex Atlanticus is preserved here and his "Portrait of a Musician" is in the Aula Leonardi.

Atellani Palace Leonardo stayed here several times, and the garden is part of the vineyard given to the artist by Ludovico il Moro.

Museo Nazionale della Scienza e della Tecnologia (see pp. 136–137) Some models made from Leonardo's drawings are displayed in a special room devoted to him, along with his model of the ideal city planned.

Palazzo Reale (see p. 45) Leonardo's first studio in Milan was in Corte Vecchia (now the Palazzo Reale), the palace of the Visconti.

AROUND PARCO SEMPIONE

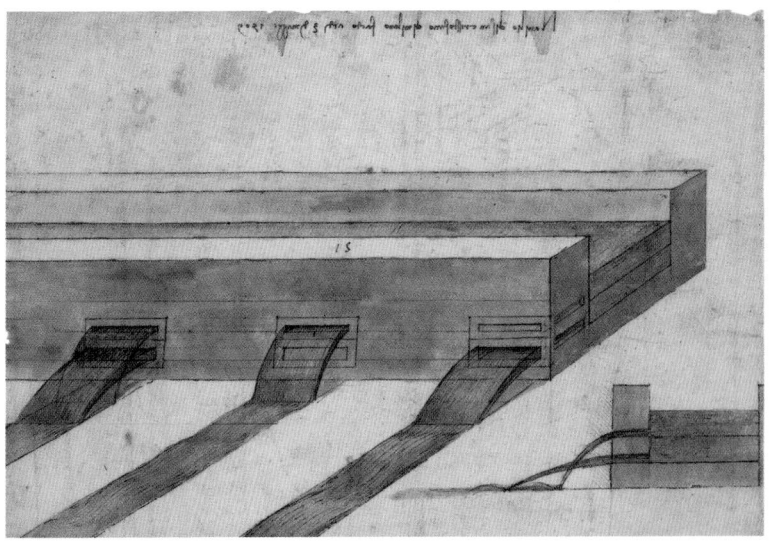

Courts, Cloisters, & Courtyards

There is so much to see behind the gates, doors, and entrances of Milan. The austere facades of churches and palaces hide wonderful architecture and greenery that often reveal the soul of the city, plantings that in spring turn every courtyard into a blossoming secret garden.

■ UNIVERSITÀ CATTOLICA

The students of the Università Cattolica are lucky; between classes they can walk beneath the colonnades of two wonderful cloisters designed by Donato Bramante, dating from 1497. One Doric and the other Ionic, they were commissioned by Ludovico il Moro from the architect when he was already working on Santa Maria delle Grazie, and were completed after he left Milan.

Largo Gemelli 1 • tel 02 72341 • Metro: Sant'Ambrogio, Line 2 • Bus: 50, 58, 94

IN **THE KNOW**

During the Giornate Nazionali ADSI, the open days of the Association of Italian Historical Dwellings, volunteers organize *cortili aperti* (open courtyards) showing people the best courtyards in Milan. Each tour concentrates on a particular area of the city, and dozens of treasures can be seen thanks to the cooperation of the owners. The free event is usually held on the last Sunday of May (*adsi.it*).

■ MUSEO DIOCESANO

Two square cloisters are all that remain of a former Dominican monastery that thrived here during the first half of the 15th century, adjacent to the Basilica di Sant'Eustorgio (see pp. 170–171). Both cloisters are elegant, tranquil places, perfect for quiet contemplation away from the hustle and bustle of the Ticinese district. The first cloister, right next to the basilica, is surrounded by columns on three sides and was restored in the 17th century. The Diocesan Museum itself is in the second cloister, rebuilt in the second half of the 20th century after being severely damaged during World War II.

Piazza Sant'Eustorgio 1 • tel 02 58101583 • Bus: 94 • Tram: 3, 9

■ ABBAZIA DI CHIARAVALLE

This 12th-century Cistercian abbey on the outskirts south of Milan is one of the earliest examples of Gothic

The courtyard of 18th-century Palazzo Morando Attendolo Bolognini on Via Sant'Andrea

AROUND PARCO SEMPIONE

architecture in Italy and still houses a community of monks. The Chiaravalle cloister was built in the 13th century, with triple arches on two sides and a beautiful rose garden in the middle. It is believed that Chiaravalle monks were the creators of the hard cheese known as Grana Padano, similar to Parmesan cheese.

Via Sant'Arialdo 102 • tel 02 57403404 • Bus: 77

■ CHIOSTRI DELL'UMANITARIA
Behind the imposing bulk of the Palazzo di Giustizia (Palace of Justice), built in the rationalist style, visitors will find

one of the most enchanting places in southeast Milan. Now the seat of the Humanitarian Society, this former Franciscan monastery of the mid-15th century boasts four cloisters: the Chiostro delle Statue, the Chiostro dei Pesci with a stone fishpond of the same date, the Chiostro delle Memorie (the smallest), and the Chiostro dei Glicini. This final one gives visitors a particularly memorable experience when its wisteria is in full and fragrant bloom. In summer the society also hosts an open-air cinema.

Via San Barnaba 48 • tel 02 5796831 • Metro: San Babila, Line 1

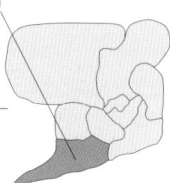

Ticinese
& Navigli

The southwestern area of Milan has two completely different sides to it, equally fascinating. The first, the inner, spiritual one, can be discovered by visiting the basilicas of San Lorenzo and Sant'Eustorgio. These are places that encourage meditation and spirituality, enhanced by the greenery of nearby Parco delle Basiliche that sets off their handsome appearance. The second side of this district is more lighthearted: The Corso di Porta Ticinese leads to the entertainment area, a triangle with Darsena as its apex and the Naviglio Grande and Naviglio Pavese as its sides. Here thrives a blend of open-air cafés, art galleries, artists' studios, and small boutiques. From this area you can leave Milan, perhaps on board a boat, or you can discover another aspect of the city beyond Porta Genova, where a former industrial district has transformed into a highly creative landscape.

◀ Seen from the air, the
Basilica di San Lorenzo
shows parts dating
back to different
ages, from the early
Christian era to the
Middle Ages.

Ticinese & Navigli

Start with the games the Romans enjoyed in the amphitheater before moving on to the interesting sites in the lively Navigli district.

8 **Chiesa di San Cristoforo** (see p. 169) Two buildings, one of the 14th century and the other of the 15th century, combine in this church, known for its frescoes. Take Via San Cristoforo and continue down Via Tortona to the museum.

9 **Museo delle Culture** (see p. 169) This museum designed by David Chipperfield houses collections and temporary exhibitions devoted to non-European cultures. End your day in the lively Via Tortona area or return to the Navigli for an *aperitivo* or dinner.

7 **Fondazione Arnaldo Pomodoro** (see p. 168) Admire exhibits of the renowned sculptor's work, along with those of other artists. Follow the Naviglio Grande for about 1.2 miles (2 km); the church will be on your right.

6 **Naviglio Grande** (see pp. 166–167) The urban stretch of this artificial canal recalls long-ago Milan. At the end of Vicolo dei Lavandai, a public washing trough until the 1950s, turn right to reach Arnaldo Pomodoro's studio.

9 Museo delle Culture

VIA VOGHERA

VIA TORTONA

VIA BERGOGNONE

ALZAIA NAVIGLIO GRANDE

DI PORTA

RIPA

TICINESE

VIA ELIA LOMBARDINI

Giardini Baden - Powell

8 Chiesa di San Cristoforo

| 0 | 200 meters |
| 0 | 200 yards |

TICINESE & NAVIGLI DISTANCE: 4.2 MILES (6.7 KM)
TIME: ABOUT 7 HOURS METRO START: MISSORI, LINE 3

TICINESE & NAVIGLI

2 Roman Amphitheater (see pp. 164–165) History buffs will enjoy the main Roman entertainment site outside the city gates. Then backtrack to the columns and turn right down Corso di Porta Ticinese. The museum will be on your left.

1 Basilica di San Lorenzo (see p. 164) Start your day at this landmark, a basilica with its monumental Roman columns and wonderful mosaics in its chapel. From the arch, cross onto Via de Amicis and go straight. Access to the amphitheater is from the cloister of Antiquarium Alda Levi at no. 17.

3 Museo Diocesano (see p. 165) Founded by Carlo Maria Martini, archbishop of Milan, this museum exhibits art treasures of the church. Next continue down Corso di Porta Ticinese.

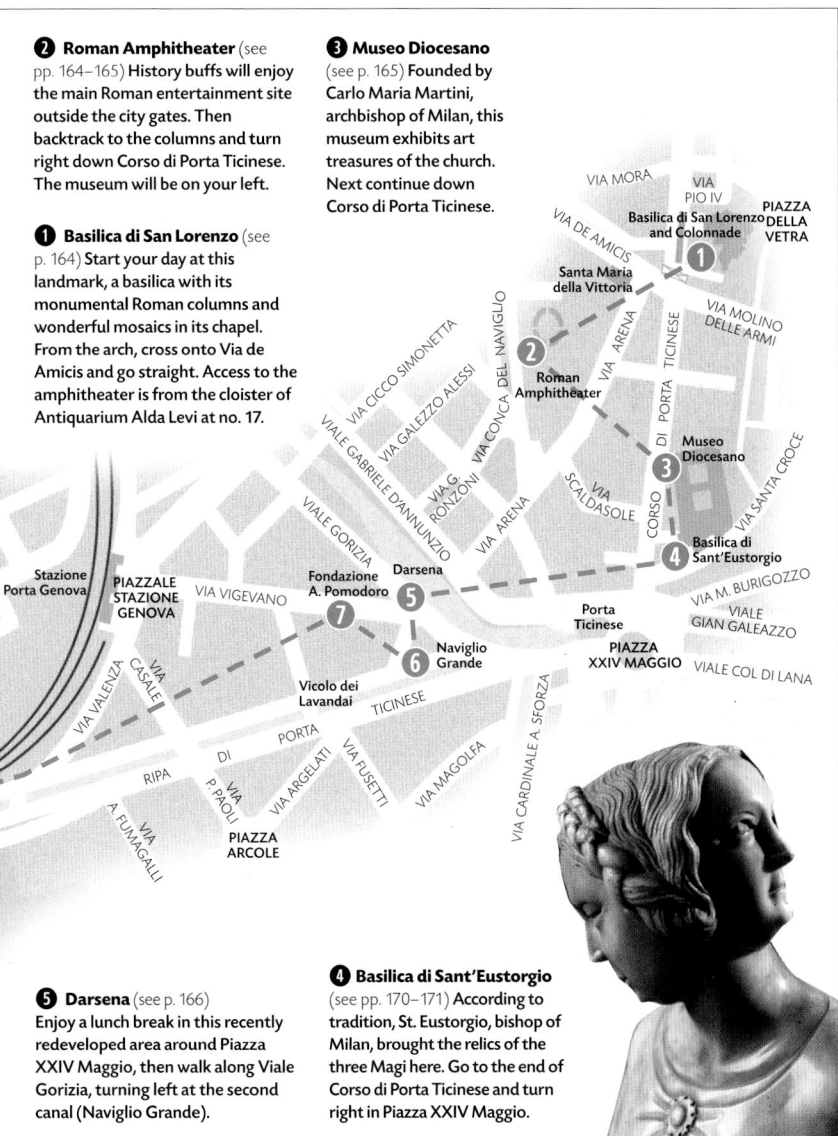

TICINESE & NAVIGLI

5 Darsena (see p. 166) Enjoy a lunch break in this recently redeveloped area around Piazza XXIV Maggio, then walk along Viale Gorizia, turning left at the second canal (Naviglio Grande).

4 Basilica di Sant'Eustorgio (see pp. 170–171) According to tradition, St. Eustorgio, bishop of Milan, brought the relics of the three Magi here. Go to the end of Corso di Porta Ticinese and turn right in Piazza XXIV Maggio.

NEIGHBORHOOD **WALK**

IN **THE KNOW**

If you want to baffle your friends, ask them how many columns there are in the San Lorenzo Colonnade. Everyone will say "16." Shake your head no and people will start wondering: Do the pillars count? Is there a hidden column? When they give up, point to the top of the colonnade where a tiny column stands, right in the center. The 17th column!

Basilica di San Lorenzo

1 Following the maxim that "everything is created, nothing is destroyed," the Basilica di San Lorenzo Maggiore was built in the fourth century on a foundation of stones taken from the outer ring of the nearby Roman amphitheater. The church, one of the first built after the Edict of Constantine, has a central plan—a square area with its sides extending into four exedras. It has withstood several rebuildings, and as a result San Lorenzo is recognized as one of the most important relics of the Roman and early Christian era. The main part of the building adjoins the **Cappella di Sant'Aquilino,** reached through a marble portal taken from a first-century monument. The octagonal chapel is the best preserved part of the church, containing wonderful fourth-century mosaics. Outside the church rises the **San Lorenzo Colonnade,** 16 Corinthian columns dating from the second or third centuries, relocated here in the fourth century for the basilica portico from an unknown pagan temple. Today they mark a favorite meeting place for young Milanese.

Corso di Porta Ticinese 35 • tel 02 89404129 • Metro: Duomo, Line 1, 3 • Bus: 94 • Tram: 2, 3, 14

Roman Amphitheater

2 The number of puzzle pieces telling the story of ancient Milan as capital of the Roman Empire is increasing every year. One of the main pieces of this puzzle, the amphitheater, was reopened to the public in 2004. After lengthy excavations, the elliptical and radial foundations of the building (built between the second and third centuries A.D.) situated in the southwestern suburb of Mediolanum near Porta Ticinese, have emerged again. Recent finds from the excavations, now exhibited in the **Antiquarium Alda Levi,** show that public executions and duels between gladiators took place here.

Via de Amicis 17 • tel 02 89400555 • Closed Sun.–Mon., Antiquarium closed Sun.–Wed. • Metro: Sant'Ambrogio, Line 2 • Bus: 94 • Tram: 3

Museo Diocesano

3 Opened in 2001 by Cardinal Carlo Maria Martini, archbishop of Milan (1972–2002), the Diocesan Museum is situated in a very important religious building, the **cloisters of Sant'Eustorgio,** the remains of a Dominican convent. They were seriously damaged during World War II but were later restored, and they remain an oasis of calm in which to quietly walk and meditate as the Dominican monks did for several centuries. Today the museum displays the artistic heritage of the diocese, with a permanent collection of more than 700 artistically and historically important works dating from the 4th to the 21st century. These consist of the collections of the archbishops of Milan, together with the Alberto Crespi collection of **gold leaf panel paintings,** dating from the 14th and 15th centuries, mainly from Tuscany. In 2014 the **drawings section** was opened, after receiving a a legacy from the Sozzani collection: 105 works dating from the 15th to the 19th centuries. An excellent craft market is held in the museum cloister twice a year, in May and October.

Corso di Porta Ticinese 95 • tel 02 89420019 • museodiocesano.it • Closed Mon., Jan. 1, May 1, Dec. 25–26 • €€, € on Tues. • Bus: 94 • Tram: 3, 9

Basilica di Sant'Eustorgio

4 See pp. 170–171.

Piazza Sant'Eustorgio 1 • tel 02 58101583 • Museum & Portinari Chapel €€ • Bus: 94 • Tram: 3, 9

A shrine marks the end of the colonnade of San Lorenzo, a popular meeting spot.

NEIGHBORHOOD **WALK**

TICINESE & NAVIGLI

GOOD **EATS**

■ AL FRESCO

A delightful restaurant in the
Tortona district where, in good
weather, you can have lunch
or dine in the open air. Kokichi
Takahashi, born in Japan but
trained in Italy, uses only fresh
ingredients in his open-plan
kitchen. **Via Savona 50,
tel 02 49533630, €€€€**

■ CANTINA DELLA VETRA

Basilica di San Lorenzo can be
seen from the big glass windows
of this warm and informal bistro,
with focus on traditional dishes
and Italian delicatessen. The
excellent brunch includes an
interesting selection of salami
and cheeses.
**Via Pio IV 3 cnr. Piazza Vetra,
tel 02 89403843, closed Mon.,
€€€€, brunch €€€**

■ CARLO E CAMILLA IN SEGHERIA

A new Navigli restaurant by
Carlo Cracco, star of *Masterchef,*
located in an old sawmill with
exposed concrete. A great place
to meet Milanese, its single large
central table seats 65 people.
The surprise is the reasonable
price. **Via Meda 24, tel 02
8373963, closed Sun., €€€€**

Darsena

5 After it evaded the threat of
being transformed into an
enormous parking lot, the area around
the old merchant port known as the
Darsena became the target of intense
revitalization in preparation for Expo
2015. When what was once the great
port of Milan, built in 1603 by the
Spanish governor, ceased operation
in the 1970s, the area became one of
the bleakest places in the city. Now
upgrading has improved the whole
district with green spaces and lively
cafés. **Piazza XXIV Maggio** has
become a largely pedestrianized zone
overlooking the Darsena, a center of
the canal network.

Metro: Porta Genova F. S., Line 2 • Tram: 3, 9

Naviglio Grande

6 The oldest artificial canal
comes from the Ticino River at
Tornavento in the province of Varese
and after 31 miles (50 km) and a
drop of 108 feet (33 m) it ends at the
Porta Ticinese in Darsena. In the last
decade this area has changed and it
is now a favorite destination for evenings out, especially in summer,
as a place to relax and feel the atmosphere of early Milan. One
particularly evocative place just off the Naviglio Grande is the **Vicolo
dei Lavandai,** the last public washing trough in Milan, where clothes
were cleaned until the 1950s. (It is named after the washermen, not the

166 | TICINESE & NAVIGLI

washerwomen, because in the 19th century a brotherhood of men was in charge of the service.) If you're visiting the Naviglio on the first Sunday of the month, you will find the crowded **Mercatone dell'Antiquariato** (antique market) in full swing, stretching from Viale Gorizia to the bridge of Via Valenza. For those with green thumbs, April brings a huge gardening event, **Fiori & Sapori sul Naviglio Grande** (Flowers and Flavor on the Naviglio Grande), when more than 200 nurserymen from all over Italy converge on the section of Naviglio closest to the Darsena.

Alzaia Naviglio Grande (street running parallel on the right-hand side of the Naviglio) & Ripa Porta Ticinese (on the left-hand side) • Metro: Porta Genova F. S., Line 2 • Tram: 3, 9

Along the Naviglio Grande, once part of an extensive network of canals

Admiring an exhibit at the Arnaldo Pomodoro Foundation

Fondazione Arnaldo Pomodoro

7 Consider a dose of contemporary art on your walk through old Milan. Arnaldo Pomodoro, an Italian sculptor and goldsmith currently living in Milan, is famous for his "sphere within a sphere" sculptures, one of which can be found in front of the United Nations building in New York. His eponymous foundation offers an attractive exhibition space with shows open to the public, located on Via Vigevano, next to the archives of the Foundation and the sculptor's studio. The exhibits draw from the Foundation's permanent collection (not open to the public), which includes more than 50 works by the artist from 1955 to today, complemented by some 30 works by other artists, from Fausto Melotti to Pietro Consagra, from Giò Pomodoro to Marco Lodola. Young artists who have taken part in the international competition for sculptors sponsored by the Foundation are also represented.

Vicolo dei Lavandai 2/a, entry from Via Vigevano 9 • tel 02 89075394 • fondazionearnaldopomodoro.it • Closed Mon.–Tues., Sat.–Sun. • Metro: Porta Genova F. S., Line 2 • Tram: 3, 9

Chiesa di San Cristoforo

8 History has often knocked at the door of St. Christopher's church, a complex consisting of two small churches built side by side along the Naviglio Grande. It is believed that it was here that Barbarossa's defeat by the Lega Lombarda (Lombard League) in Legnano was announced in 1176. To commemorate the end of the plague in 1339, and to fulfill a vow, the inhabitants erected the church on the right (usually known as the **Cappella Ducale**), at the request of Gian Galeazzo Visconti. It was at St. Christopher's that another Milanese nobleman, Ludovico il Moro, sought to meet his young bride Beatrice d'Este, brought to him from Ferrara. The church on the left is the older one, with a beautiful **brick portal,** while the right facade is adorned with the Visconti and Milanese coats of arms set between two single-lancet windows. When the adjoining wall was knocked down in 1625, the two churches became one, forming the two-nave interior decorated with **frescoes** by the school of Bergognone and Bernardino Luini as well as precious **wooden sculptures,** including a St. Christopher from the 14th century, in the left nave.

Via San Cristoforo 3 • tel 02 48951413 • Tram: 2

Museo delle Culture

9 Known as MUDEC, this new museum inhabits a huge area once belonging to the Ansaldo factory, where zinc-sheathed boxy buildings are counterbalanced by curving walls of glass. The renovation is the work of architect David Chipperfield, whose vision for the museum complex won a design competition. Perhaps most noticeable is the central quatrefoil crystal structure that is always lit, a lantern for the city at night. **Città delle Culture** hosts temporary exhibitions as well as collections from the storerooms of the Castello Sforzesco. In addition to exhibition areas, there is space for educational workshops, an auditorium, a bookshop, and on the top floor, a restaurant.

Via Tortona 56 • tel 02 54917 • mudec.it • Metro: Porta Genova F. S., Line 2 • Bus: 47, 68, 74, 90/91 • Tram: 2, 9, 14, 19

> ### SAVVY **TRAVELER**
>
> **Departing from Alzaia Naviglio 4, the minicruise Itinerario delle Conche** (*naviglilombardi.it*) **follows a historic route along the Milanese canals. Among the stops: Vicolo dei Lavandai, Chiesa di San Cristoforo, the bridge of the Scodellino (little bowl), the Darsena, and Naviglio Pavese as far as the Conchetta lock.**

Basilica di Sant'Eustorgio

Behind its neo-Romanesque facade is a Renaissance masterpiece and an early Christian necropolis, as well as the relics of the three Magi.

Sant'Eustorgio church is where St. Barnabas may have baptized the first Christians.

The importance attached to the Basilica di Sant'Eustorgio by the city of Milan arises from the fact that archbishops traditionally entered the city through the Porta Ticinese, making their first stop this basilica founded by Eustorgius I in the 4th century to preserve the relics of the Magi. A Romanesque church was built here in the 11th century, and later rebuilt after its destruction by Barbarossa. In the Gothic period, family chapels were added on the right side and the neo-Romanesque brick facade was constructed in 1865.

■ Cappella Portinari

The undisputed masterpiece at the Basilica di Sant'Eustorgio is the Portinari Chapel, commissioned by Pigello Portinari, a Florentine nobleman and banker, and built in the second half of the 15th century to contain his own tomb as well as the relics of St. Peter Martyr. The chapel, built on a central plan in the Florentine style, is decorated in parts with frescoes by Vincenzo Foppa, depicting "Scenes From the Life of St. Peter" and the "Life of the Virgin"; the tambour in the cupola boasts a terra-cotta high-relief depicting angels dancing, while its ribs are decorated with polychrome shells, colored with concentric stripes. As you leave the basilica, notice the commemorative stone on the left of the facade noting the site where St. Barnabas supposedly baptized the first Milanese, giving rise to Christianity here.

■ Two Traditions

April 29 is the feast of St. Peter of Verona, also known as St. Peter Martyr. On that day people suffering from migraines come to this church to pay homage to the saint's relics; he was killed when the top of his head was

IN **THE KNOW**

Take a close look at the bell tower of Sant'Eustorgio, built starting in 1297. It houses the most ancient public clock in Italy. You will not find the usual cross at the top of the tower, but an eight-pointed star, representing the star that led the Magi to the Holy Child.

cut off with an ax and it is said that on touching his urn, your headache will disappear. Another tradition associated with Sant'Eustorgio is that of the **Corteo dei Magi** (Procession of the Three Kings) at Epiphany. It starts at the Piazza Duomo, arriving at the basilica after a stop at San Lorenzo, where the Three Kings meet Herod and his court in a reenactment.

■ The Necropolis

In the 1950s, during excavations under the nave of the early medieval cathedral, the ruins of an early Christian necropolis were found together with tombs of the Augustan age, and a great number of epigraphs, the most famous known as the "prayer's epitaph." Today the necropolis and the Cappella Portinari are both accessible with a single ticket from the basilica's museum; enter to the left of the church.

TICINESE & NAVIGLI

Piazza Sant'Eustorgio 1 • tel 02 58101583 • Museum & Portinari Chapel €€ • Bus: 94 • Tram: 3, 9

City of Design

Function, aesthetics, communication, industry: These are the ingredients of design that Milan has combined with such skill that it is now rightly known as the capital of Italian design. The claim covers more than fashionable apparel, as evidenced by showrooms and studios devoted to interior, industrial and product design, and the way even the design of the most humble everyday objects is given respectful consideration.

TICINESE & NAVIGLI

Above and opposite: Displays at the Salone Internazionale del Mobile, the fabulous annual international furniture fair

Between Salone and Fuorisalone

April in Milan is synonymous with furniture and design. The main event is the huge **Salone Internazionale del Mobile** (International Furniture Fair; *salonemilano.it*) that takes place at the Milan exhibition center in Rho. A parallel show, **Salone Satellite,** displays the work of designers under age 35, in two pavilions. Then there are the events and festivities of the concurrent **Fuorisalone** (Design Week; *fuorisalone.it*), attracting design professionals as well as avid fans of the genre. The Università Statale (State University) hosts some of the most spectacular installations, but there are exciting things to be seen in other districts of the city as well.

Achille Castiglioni's Studio and Museum

After the death of famed industrial designer Achille Castiglioni, known for his use of ordinary materials and clean lines, his studio was converted into a museum and is now open for guided tours (*Piazza Castello 27, tel 02 8053606, closed Sat.– Mon., reservations required*). In the beautiful rooms overlooking Castello Sforzesco are prototypes, scale models, drawing boards, and various objects collected by Castiglioni throughout his life. Be sure to visit the conference room, which holds the items bearing his creative stamp that have also marked the history of design, such as the Arco Lamp.

Design Shops

In Milan, design has settled in the center. The largest concentration of showrooms is along **Via Durini,** with names such as Cassina, B&B, Poltrona Frau, and Porro, while **Corso Monforte** has become the center of lighting, with shops such as Artemide, FontanaArte, Luceplan, and Flos. Of note on the nearby **Corso Venezia** is De Padua, a must for all design and furnishing enthusiasts. New trends in design and lifestyle are on view at the **Design Supermarket,** a concept store in the basement of the department store La Rinascente *(Via Santa Radegonda 3).*

TICINESE & NAVIGLI

Getting Away From the City

If you can travel just a few miles outside of Milan, you will be delighted to discover such treasures as the Reggia and Duomo of Monza, the medieval charm of Bergamo Alta, the historic villas around Lake Como, and the amazing gardens and palazzi of the Borromean Islands on Lake Maggiore.

TICINESE & NAVIGLI

■ MONZA

Monza, the capital of the Monza and Brianza Province, is only 12 miles (20 km) away from Milan, with frequent trains from Centrale and Garibaldi Stations. Here at the end of the 18th century, Maria Theresa of Austria entrusted the architect Piermarini with the task of building a palace as a country house for her son Ferdinand I. The resulting grand **Villa Reale** (Royal Villa; *Viale Brianza 1, Monza, tel 039 464213*) has 740 rooms, recently restored. The complex includes extensive gardens and parks, set over 1,700 acres (700 ha), making it one of the largest historic parks in Europe. In the center of Monza, make a point to see the **Duomo** and its **museum,** notably the **Corona Ferrea** (Iron Crown). According to ancient tradition, this crown is linked to the Passion of Christ, and it was used for crowning the kings of Italy until the 19th century, lastly by Napoleon. It is on display in the **Cappella di Teodolinda,** below magnificent frescoes by the Zavattari. If you are driving your own automobile, take it for a spin on the **Autodromo di Monza,** where the F1 Grand Prix is held.

■ BERGAMO ALTA

Completed in 1588, the 3.7-mile (6 km) walls erected by the Venetians still enclose the upper and oldest part of the city, known as Bergamo Alta. Reached by funicular (or a 30-minute uphill walk), this historic center is a delight to discover on foot, a medieval town with towers and campaniles often compared with those of Tuscany. At its center is the **Piazza Vecchia** and the **Palazzo della Ragione,** dating from the Renaissance, and the **Piazza del Duomo,** where the Duomo, the **Basilica of Santa Maria Maggiore,** and the 15th-century **Cappella Colleoni** all vie for attention. Trains from Milan's Centrale and Garibaldi Stations generally travel to and from Bergamo hourly.

A view of the Lecco arm of Lake Como, reaching through the peaks of Monte Barro

■ Lake Como

The impressive villas and gardens around lovely Lake Como are best appreciated from the water. Luckily, excellent boat service *(navigazionelaghi.it)* links the surrounding towns, making for easy exploring. From Milan's Cadorna Station, take the train to Como Lago.

■ Borromean Islands

This amazing archipelago in the middle of Lake Maggiore includes islands where the Borromeo family began erecting magnificent palaces, set in the most enchanting gardens, beginning in the 16th century. Today they are accessible to visitors from Milan via train to Stresa, the main hub, from which frequent ferries travel to the various islands *(seasonal openings, isoleborromee.it)*. **Isola Bella** is almost entirely filled by a sumptuous baroque palace, surrounded by an Italian-style garden. Don't miss its picture gallery. The **Isola Madre** is known for its romantic English-style garden and 16th-century palazzo with well-restored period rooms. The **Isola dei Pescatori,** the smallest, is the only one that is inhabited year-round, and offers restaurants specializing in dishes prepared with fish from the lake.

PART 3

Travel Essentials

PLANNING YOUR TRIP

The Milan tourism website *turismo.milano.it* offers services and information about everything that might be useful to organize your trip and make the most of your stay in the city. Information is available in English and Italian, with some sections also available in five other languages.

When to Go

The best times to visit Milan are in autumn between September and November, when the weather is still quite mild, and in spring from March to May. June and July, although hot, are ideal times to enjoy nightlife and take part in the many open-air events. Note that in August, especially the two weeks in the middle of the month, most shops and restaurants are closed for vacation. Before planning your visit check to see when Fashion and Design Weeks take place, as the city will be more crowded and hotel prices much higher. If you are not visiting for these special events, you may wish to come another time.

Climate

In winter the weather in Milan is cold and damp, with temperatures ranging between 30°F and 50°F (-2°C–8°C). The hottest and most humid months are June and July, with temperatures ranging between 59°F and 77°F (15°C–25°C).

What to Take

You should be able to buy everything you need in Milan. Pharmacies offer a wide range of drugs, medical supplies, and toiletries, along with expert advice, but you should bring any prescription drugs you might need. Many brand-name drugs are different in Italy. A pharmacy *(famacia)* is indicated by a green cross outside the store. It is also useful to bring a second pair of glasses or contact lenses if you wear them.

Clothing will depend on when you travel and the activities you plan. Italians generally dress more smartly than most U.S., Canadian, and northern European visitors. Make some effort for any meal out, and always dress appropriately in churches—ideally no bare shoulders or shorts for women. Bring a sweater, even in summer, for evenings can be chilly.

Electricity in Italy is 220V, and plugs have two (sometimes three) round pins. If you bring electrical equipment, you will need a plug adapter plus a transformer for U.S. appliances.

Finally, don't forget the essentials: passport, driver's license, tickets, traveler's checks, credit cards, and insurance documents. When staying in a hotel you will have to give documents such as ID and passports to the hotel reception. They will look after the required registration with the police. This is mandatory, even for a single night in a hotel.

HOW TO GET TO MILAN

Passports

U.S. and Canadian citizens need a passport to enter Italy for stays of up to 90 days. No visa is required.

By Plane

Milan has three international airports: **Forlanini–Milano Linate,** 4.3 miles (7 km) east of Milan; **Milan–Malpensa,** 31 miles (50 km) northwest of the city; and **Caravaggio–Bergamo Orio al Serio,** 28 miles (45 km) northeast of Milan.

Getting to the City Center

From Forlanini–Milano Linate: ATM runs bus no. 73 every ten minutes from the airport to Piazza San Babila (40 minutes). Route 4 of the Metro is currently under construction, with estimated completion in 2020; eventually it will link Linate to San Cristoforo F. S.

For private car service from Linate, **Consorzio Fly Car Service** *(tel 02 70208021, linateflycarservice.com)* has a desk at Arrivals, gate 6. Cost for seven people to central Milan is around €300; a taxi should cost €20 to €30.

From Malpensa: Milan's major intercontinental airport, Milan–Malpensa *(flight* information, tel 02 232323, sea-aeroportimilano.it), is an impractical 31 miles (50 km) northwest of the city center. A dedicated rail link, the **Malpensa Express** (tel 800 500005, www.malpensaexpress.it), has 51 daily trips to and from Milano Centrale (43 minutes) and 78 daily services to and from Milano Cadorna (29 to 36 minutes). Tickets are about €12.

Bus services between the Stazione Centrale (Central Station) and the airport are provided by **Malpensa Shuttle** (malpensashuttle.it) and by **Malpensa Bus Express** (stie.it), both with departures every 20 minutes. Cost is about €10.

At Malpensa **Consorzio European Limousine** (tel 346 9719841, europeanlimousine.it) is at Terminal 1, level B Arrivals, gate 6. Cost to transport seven people in a limo to central Milan is around €450 from Malpensa.

Cabs outside Arrivals are plentiful, but be sure to take a licensed taxi. A taxi from Malpensa to central Milan should cost around €90.

From Caravaggio–Bergamo Orio al Serio: Links between this airport and Milan Central Station are provided by **Autostradale** (autostradale.it), **Orio Shuttle** (orioshuttle.com), and **Terravision** (terravision.eu). Cost is about €5 by bus. A taxi from Bergamo to central Milan costs about €150.

GETTING AROUND MILAN

By Bicycle

Milan currently has 87 miles (140 km) of cycle lanes, of which 80 percent are on the roads. For short journeys (maximum 2 hours) the bike-sharing service **BikeMi** (tel 02 48607607, bikemi.it) allows you to pick up a bike and take it back to any docking station in the city. There are annual and weekly subscriptions, as well as daily tickets that can be purchased online, by smartphone, from ATM Points, or by calling the ATM Infoline (tel 02 48607607). Rental is free for the first 30 minutes. Subscribers must be at least 16 years old.

By Car

It is easy to rent a car in Italy, although costs are high by U.S. standards. It may be worth arranging car rental before leaving home. Cheaper deals in Italy can often be found through smaller local companies—look under Autonoleggio. Drivers must be over 21 and hold a full license to rent a car.

Since 2012 **Area C** has been introduced to regulate vehicle access to the historic center of Milan. It is in force on weekdays from 7:30 a.m. to 7:30 p.m. (on Thursdays only until 6 p.m.). To drive your car in Area C you must pay a congestion charge

before midnight of the day following your entering the ZTL (Zona a Traffico Limitato), or by a deferred payment within seven days after entering the ZTL.

By Public Transportation

The simplest way to get around the city is by bus, tram, or the Metropolitana (subway). Milan has four metro lines: M1: Linea Rossa/Red Line, M2: Linea Verde/Green Line, M3: Linea Gialla/Yellow Line, and M5: Linea Lilla/Lilac Line. (The M4: Linea Blu/Blue Line is under construction.) Depending on your needs, you can buy a single city ticket (€1.50); a pack of ten tickets, called a carnet (€13.80, cannot be used by more than one person at the same time); a day ticket (€4.50), or a two-day ticket (€8.25). Note: To get to the Rho Fiera exhibition center you must buy an extra-urban ticket. When accompanied by an adult with a valid ticket, children under the age of ten travel free (there is a maximum of two children per adult).

Tickets can be bought at **ATM Points** (tel 02 48607607, atm.it), at authorized sales outlets (bars, tobacconists, stationers, and newsstands), and from automatic ticket machines in the Metro. All the ATM Points and authorized sales outlets also sell **RicaricaMi**, a rechargeable electronic card for weekly tickets, day tickets, a pack of ten tickets, and ordinary tickets.

ATM Points are at:
Metro stop Duomo
Metro stop Loreto
Metro stop Stazione Cadorna
Metro stop Stazione Centrale
Metro stop Stazione Garibaldi
Metro stop Stazione Romolo

Milan is also served by the **Passante railway** (marked on Metro maps as "S" Lines). This is an underground railway connecting with suburban lines fanning out in all directions from the city to the suburbs and the rest of Lombardy. It's essentially a commuter train but can be used within the city as well. There are 13 S lines in total. The urban section (from Porta Vittoria, where the LIN shuttle bus from Linate leaves passengers) can be accessed with a valid public transport ticket.

The **Radiobus di Quartiere** or **District Radiobus** (tel 02 48034803, atm.it/en) is a night bus operating daily from 10 p.m. until 2 a.m. It picks up passengers at designated terminus points throughout the city; alternatively a passenger can telephone shortly before going to the stop or book it after 1 p.m. on the same day.

By Sightseeing Tour

One sightseeing option, **City Tour** (tel 02 867131) offers a 3.5-hour cultural tour of the city with multilingual guides to help you discover the main attractions of the city. The bus tours run from Tuesday through Sunday, departing at 9:30 a.m. and ending at 1 p.m. in Foro Buonaparte.

Independent Sightseeing

City Sightseeing (tel 02 867131, milano.city-sightseeing .it) offers 90-minute itineraries that include the main tourist sights in Milan in a double-decker open-topped bus with commentary in eight languages.

In addition, there are also many associations that organize theme walks and tours, such as:

Ad Artem,
adartem.it
Artema,
gruppoartema.it
Centro guide turistiche di Milano,
centroguidemilano.net
Clessidra,
associazioneclessidra.it
Leonardo a Milano,
leonardoamilano.org
Milano città nascosta,
cittanascostamilano.it
Milano guida,
milanoguida.com
Milano4You,
milanofouryou.it
Neiade,
visiteguidatemilano.com
Urbansafari,
urbansafaritour.it
Viaggi di Architettura,
viaggidiarchitettura.it

By Taxi

Taxis are available at taxi stands. The fare is determined exclusively by the taxi meter, which has a fixed starting charge that varies depending on whether it is day or nighttime or a holiday; then a set amount is added for each kilometer

(0.6 mile) of the journey. The first piece of luggage is free. Tipping is optional. To call a radiotaxi: Arco (tel 02 6767), Autoradio Taxi (tel 02 8585), Cooperativa Esperia (tel 02 8383), Cooperativa tassisti associati (tel 02 3490809), Etaxi (tel 02 5353), La Fontana Soc. Coop. A.R.L. Taxi Centro Servizi (tel 02 3492063), Soc. Coop. Arl. (tel 02 85871), Taxi Blu (tel 02 4040), Yellow Taxi (tel 02 6969).

By Train

Milan is the main railway junction in northern Italy. The national and international services are run by **Trenitalia** (trenitalia.com), while **Trenord** (trenord.it) runs the suburban and regional services; the Malpensa Express services from the airport (from Milano Cadorna to Milano Centrale, Milano Porta, and Garibaldi) and the cross-border services Como–Chiasso and Malpensa–Bellinzona. Milan has 22 stations and railway stops. The main ones are Stazione Centrale, Stazione Garibaldi, Stazione Lambrate, and Stazione Cadorna, all connected to the metro.

PRACTICAL ADVICE

Apps

Milan's website for tourists, **turismo.milano.it,** strives to inform about all the events organized in the city through the app **Eventi**

Milano, available for iPhone, iPod Touch, Android and WindowsPhone, iTunes, and Google Play.

Guida Milano is like having a guidebook straight on your phone. It offers 13 itineraries around the city, each of them focused on a different theme, including the city center; historical time period such as Ancient Rome, Baroque, and Neoclassical; and churches, palazzi, and parks. The last itinerary focuses on sites beyond the city. This app is available in five languages (Italian, English, Spanish, Russian, and Chinese), for iPhone/iPad and Android.

Milano Itinerari is an app that suggests itineraries and provides information about places to visit in Milan, based on your particular areas of interest. The itineraries and sites are organized by subject (shopping, wine and food, history, art, etc.) and by category (architecture, museums, parks, etc.). The app also enables you to create your own itineraries and to save your preferences on the device. It is available for iPhone/iPad and Android.

Milano Musei is dedicated to Milan's museums, allowing users to learn which ones are closest to their location, along with info on exhibits, opening times, and ticket prices. Available for iPhone/iPad and Android.

Bargains

On special occasions, such as during the Salone del Mobile (Furniture Fair), entrance to the city museums is free. Museums are also free during the Notte dei Musei (Night of the Museums), usually held mid-May. It is also worth mentioning that the Gallerie d'Italia and Casa Boschi Di Stefano always offer free admission, and the Museo del Novecento is free for those under the age of 25. On Tuesday the entrance to the Museo Diocesano is half price. On Wednesday cinema tickets are reduced throughout the city.

Consulates

A complete list of consulates is available on the Milan tourist website *turismo.milano.it*

Money Matters

To change money, go to a major bank or a storefront exchange office (look for the *"cambio"* sign). For the best exchange rate, however, use your debit or credit card at one of the many ATMs in the city.

Banks are usually open from 8:30 a.m. to 1:30 p.m. and from 2:30 to 3 or 4 p.m. They are closed on Saturday and Sunday.

Opening Times

The opening hours of shops vary enormously from district to district and depend on the type of shop. In Milan food shops are usually closed on Monday afternoon while other shops are usually closed Monday morning. There are, however, an increasing number of supermarkets open every day, until late. In the center of the city, shops are usually open from 10 a.m. to 7:30 p.m. while elsewhere they close for lunch from 1 p.m. to 3:30 p.m.

Many shops close in August, some for two weeks, others for the whole month.

Public Holidays

January 1 and 6, Easter Sunday, Easter Monday, April 25, May 1, June 2, August 15, November 1, December 7 (Milan only), 8, 25, and 26.

Restrooms

Milan has few public restrooms, but bars and cafés usually let you use theirs. One toilet often serves both men and women. Standards of hygiene vary and it's a good idea to carry tissues, as toilet paper isn't always guaranteed.

Telephones

To call Italy from the United States, dial 011 39 (international and Italian country code) then the local number, which always includes the city area code: 02 for Milan. This goes for in-city calls as well. Be aware that, not counting the area codes, Italian phone numbers can have from four digits (government offices, some embassies) to eight digits. 800 and 848 numbers are toll free; 199 numbers have a higher rate. For directory assistance, call

1254. To make a collect call, dial 170. Public phones are operated by phone cards, which can be bought at tobacconists, bars, and post offices.

Time Differences

Italy is six hours ahead of New York, NY, nine hours ahead of Los Angeles, CA, and one hour ahead of London, England. In Europe, clocks move forward one hour on the last Sunday of March and return to standard time on the last Sunday in October.

Tipping

In restaurants where a service charge (servizio) is not levied, leave 10 to 15 percent; even where it is, you may wish to leave 5 to 10 percent for the waiter. In bars, tip a few cents for drinks consumed standing at bars, and 25c to 50c for waiter service. In hotel bars be slightly more generous.

Service is included in hotel rates, but tip chambermaids and doormen about 50c (€1 for calling a cab), the bellhop €1 to €3 for carrying your bags, and the concierge or porter €3 to €7 if he or she has been helpful. Double these figures for the most expensive hotels.

Tip restroom and checkroom attendants up to 25c. Porters at airports and railroad stations generally work to fixed tariffs, but tip up to €2 extra at your discretion. Cab drivers expect around 10 percent. Barbers merit around €2. Tip church or other custodians €1 to €2.

Tourist Offices

Consult the helpful tourist website *turismo.milano.it* before going to an information office in case there are changes.
IAT: Piazza Castello, cnr. Via Beltrami, tel 02 77404343
IAT: Stazione Centrale Binario 21, tel 02 77404318

Travelers With Disabilities

To enable people in wheelchairs to reach the various levels in Metro stations, there are 81 electric stair lifts with mobile platforms (the existence of a stair lift is indicated outside the station by the appropriate symbol). Some stations also have elevators. Before setting off it is important to check the ATM website *(atm.it)* or call the Infoline *(tel 02 48607607)*. On aboveground stops, the routes of some lines are served by carriages with lowered floors adapted for wheelchair use. In addition to being wider, they are the same height as the platform to make wheelchair access much easier; they are also fitted with LOGES paths (a distinctive surface that can be felt with the feet) along the edge of the platform for the visually impaired. To provide continuity, the sidewalks near these stops have been fitted with slopes at street crossings. Metro cars adapted for wheelchairs are labeled with the international symbol for motor disability (a white wheelchair on a blue background) to indicate the

carriage with a place reserved for the disabled, fitted with an anchorage system to ensure safety. All city buses, the new trolleybuses, and the new city trams are fitted with lowered platforms, so there are no steps to get in and out, as well as a pull-out ramp and a space reserved for the disabled.

Wi-Fi

Open Wifi Milano
(info.openwifimilano.it) is the City of Milan's free wireless network. The service enables you to surf the Net in all the parts of the city covered by the service. There are currently 500 hotspots in more than 250 places. The free service provided by the city inside some public buildings is called **Free Wi-Fi Indoor** and it is available during the opening hours of more than 50 city buildings, including libraries, registry offices, and museums.

EMERGENCIES

Emergency Telephone Numbers

24-hour pharmacy:
02 6690735
Ambulance/emergency medical assistance:
118
Fire: *115*
Police: *113*
Carabinieri (military police):
112
U.S. Consulate: *02 290351*

HOTELS

Milan is flush with numerous luxury hotels, magnificent palazzi furnished with beautiful antique furniture. But there are also more modest establishments, less formal and family run. The following list of hotels is simply a sampling of what is available; take a look and choose what would suit you best. As Milan is quite a small city, you will never be too far from the main tourist sites, but it makes sense to stay in a hotel near areas you particularly want to visit. Although accommodations in Milan can be very expensive, there are good deals even in high season as long as you book well in advance, preferably through the hotel's website.

A complete list of Milan's accommodation facilities can be found on *turismo.milano.it.* The hotels suggested below have been selected by the author. Given the relative scarcity of good, reasonably priced accommodations in Milan, it is best to reserve as much in advance as possible to secure your preference. You'll probably be asked for a deposit or credit card number.

Street parking is difficult to find in the historic center, but if you have a car, most hotels will help arrange for you to use a garage—for which you will usually have to pay an additional daily charge. It's a good idea to inquire in advance about parking if you know you're going to need it.

Grading System

Italian hotels are rated from one to five stars by the government's tourist office according to such facilities as the number of rooms with private bathrooms, and rooms with TV and other amenities, rather than style or comfort. However, this is not always a reliable measure as, for tax reasons, many hotels opt to stay in a lower category. Unless otherwise noted, all the hotels listed here have private bathrooms in all rooms (upper categories have bathtub and shower; lower, only shower). English is spoken at all the hotels listed. Value-added tax and service are included in the prices, and so is breakfast, unless otherwise noted. Room price categories are given only for guidance and do not take seasonal variations into account.

Organization

Hotels listed here have been grouped first according to neighborhood, then listed alphabetically by price range.

Price Range

An indication of the cost of a double room in the high season is given by € signs.

€€€€€	Over €320
€€€€	€250–€320
€€€	€175–€250
€€	€85–€175
€	Under €85

Text symbols

- **①** No. of Guest Rooms
- **🚇** Public Transportation **P** Parking
- **⬍** Elevator **❄** Air-Conditioning
- **🏋** Health Club **≋** Outdoor Pool
- **⊕** Closed **◈** Credit Cards

SAN BABILA TO THE GALLERIA

■ Four Seasons
€€€€€
VIA GESÙ 6/8
TEL 02 77088
FAX 02 77085000
fourseasons.com
A luxury hotel set in a former 15th-century convent in a ritzy district, the Quadrilatero della Moda (the Fashion District).
① 118 **P** ⬍ ❄ 🏋 ≋
All major cards

■ Townhouse 8
€€€€€
VIA SILVIO PELLICO 8
TEL 02 36594690
townhouse.it
Luxury boutique hotel with only a few rooms and a magnificent view of the mosaics of the Galleria Vittorio Emanuele II.
① 11 ⬍ ❄ ◈ *All major cards*

■ Hotel Manzoni
€€€€
VIA SANTO SPIRITO 20
TEL 02 76005700
hotelmanzoni.com
Four stars in the Fashion District and an excellent quality/price ratio.
① 45 **P** ⬍ ❄ 🏋
◈ *All major cards*

■ San Pietro all'Orto 6
€€€€
VIA SAN PIETRO ALL'ORTO 6
TEL 02 781147
allegroitalia.it
Four luxury suites only a few feet from Montenapoleone, with first-class cuisine and service sure to make you feel at home.
ⓘ 4 🔄 💺 🔗 All major cards

LA SCALA & AROUND

■ Armani Hotel Milano
€€€€€
VIA MANZONI 31
TEL 02 88838888
milan.armanihotels.com
Hospitality Giorgio Armani–style in the very center of Milan. Spectacular view from the restaurant and lounge-bar windows.
ⓘ 95 🔄 💺 🔧 🔗 All major cards

■ Bulgari
€€€€€
VIA PRIVATA FRATELLI GABBA 7/B
TEL 02 8058051
bulgarihotels.com
Central and yet very quiet, the hotel has two great advantages: a private garden that is the natural extension of the nearby Botanic Garden and a spa that is one of the best in the city.
ⓘ 58 🅿 🔄 💺 🔧 🔗 All major cards

■ Milano Scala
€€€€
VIA DELL'ORSO 7
TEL 02 870961
hotelmilanoscala.it
Music and its champions are the inspiration for this recently opened four-star hotel. In summer guests enjoy their

aperitivo on the panoramic terrace on the eighth floor.
ⓘ 62 🔄 💺 🔧 🔗 All major cards

■ Cavour
€€€
VIA FATEBENEFRATELLI 21
TEL 02 620001
FAX 02 6592263
hotelcavour.it
This comfortable, traditional hotel between Via Manzoni and Brera has been completely renovated, including offering hypoallergenic rooms.
ⓘ 121 🔄 💺 🔗 All major cards

AROUND THE GIARDINI PUBBLICI

■ Hotel Manin
€€€€
VIA DANIELE MANIN 7
TEL 02 6596511
hotelmanin.it
With the Giardini Pubblici on one side and a courtyard garden on the other, this traditional, recently renovated hotel is a haven of comfort and tranquillity.
ⓘ 118 🔄 💺 🔧 🔗 All major cards

■ Sheraton Diana Majestic
€€€€
VIALE PIAVE 42
TEL 02 20581
sheratondianamajestic.com
This elegant hotel, in one of the most beautiful art nouveau palaces, is known for its courtyard garden, a very popular evening meeting point.
ⓘ 106 🔄 💺 🔧 🔗 All major cards

■ Foresteria Monforte
€€€
PIAZZA TRICOLORE 2
TEL 02 370272
foresteriamonforte.it

This pleasant and comfortable bed-and-breakfast, only ten minutes' walk from Piazza San Babila, is perfect for anyone wishing to visit Milan. As an additional bonus, a communal kitchen is available to guests.
ⓘ 3 🔄 💺 🔗 All major cards

■ NH Milano Touring
€€
VIA TARCHETTI 2
TEL 02 63351
nh-hotels.it
Recently renovated, this cozy and comfortable hotel is conveniently located near the Giardini Pubblici and Stazione Centrale.
ⓘ 282 🔄 💺 🔗 All major cards

SOUTHEAST MILAN

■ Petit Palais
€€€
VIA MOLINO DELLE ARMI 1
TEL 02 584891
petitpalais.it
French in name and style, this small, charming hotel is a romantic retreat located in the heart of the Navigli area.
ⓘ 18 🔄 💺 🔗 All major cards

■ Ca' Monteggia
€€
VIA SANT'ANTONIO 9
TEL 327 2928781
camonteggia.it
A small number of comfortable rooms, tastefully furnished, along with a communal drawing room, set in an 11th-century palazzo close to the Ca' Granda.
ⓘ 4 💺 🔗 AE, MC, V

■ Hotel Romana Residence
€€
CORSO DI PORTA ROMANA 64
TEL 02 583421

TRAVEL ESSENTIALS

hotelromanaresidence.it
Friendly and centrally located.
🏨 66 ⬆ 📶 🅿 *All major cards*

■ Uptown Palace
€€
VIA SANTA SOFIA 10
TEL 02 305131
uptownpalace.com
This modern and comfortable
business hotel/conference center
is a great value for the money.
🏨 158 🅿 ⬆ 📶 📺 🏊
📶 *All major cards*

BRERA & GARIBALDI

■ Palazzo Parigi
€€€€€
CORSO DI PORTA NUOVA 1
TEL 02 625625
palazzoparigi.com
A luxurious hotel only steps away
from the church of San Marco.
Traditional furnishings, gourmet
restaurant, and a small garden
complete the picture.
🏨 65 🅿 ⬆ 📶 📺 🏊 📶
All major cards

■ Locanda Resentin
€€€
VIA MERCATO 24
TEL 02 875923
resentin.com
With four rooms named
after the nearby streets—Fiori
Chiari, Fiori Oscuri, Brera, and
Madonnina—decorated in neutral
colors and elegant details. Its
historical café is owned by the
singer Eros Ramazzotti.
🏨 4 📶 📶 *All major cards*

■ Maison Moschino
€€€
VIALE MONTE GRAPPA 12
TEL 02 29009858
maisonmoschino.com

This hotel with its surreal decor
is much appreciated for its
friendliness. It is set in the former
railway station that linked Milan
to Monza in the 19th century.
🏨 65 ⬆ 📶 📶 *All major cards*

■ Locanda Resentin
€€€
VIA MERCATO 24
TEL 02 875923
resentin.com
With four rooms named
after the nearby streets—Fiori
Chiari, Fiori Oscuri, Brera,
and Madonnina—decorated
in neutral colors and elegant
details. Today its historical café
is owned by the singer Eros
Ramazzotti.
🏨 4 📶 📶 *All major cards*

■ La Favia Four Rooms
€€
VIA CARLO FARINI 4
TEL 347 7842212
lafavia4rooms.com
An apartment with a pretty
roof garden, very tastefully
converted to a bed-and-breakfast.
The rooms are all different and
reflect the owners' love of travel
and design.
🏨 4 📶 📶 *All major cards*

TORRE VELASCA TO PIAZZA AFFARI

■ Hotel dei Cavalieri
€€€€
PIAZZA GIUSEPPE MISSORI 1
TEL 02 88571
hoteldeicavalieri.com
This traditional hotel, situated
between the Duomo and Porta
Romana, offers a magnificent
panoramic terrace on the tenth

floor, perfect for an *aperitivo*.
🏨 167 ⬆ 📶 📶 *All major cards*

■ Spadari al Duomo
€€€€
VIA SPADARI 11
TEL 02 72002371
www.spadarihotel.com
A comfortable hotel near the
Duomo and Santa Maria presso
San Satiro.
🏨 40 ⬆ 📶 📶 *All major cards*

■ Gran Duca di York
€€€
VIA MONETA 1
TEL 02 874863
ducadiyork.com
A small number of rooms,
recently renovated, set in an
18th-century palace in the stock
exchange district.
🏨 33 ⬆ 📶 📶 *All major cards*

■ bbMilanoDuomo
€€
VIA TORINO 46
TEL 347 7796170
This quiet bed-and-breakfast,
overlooking a courtyard, is set
in a 19th-century palazzo on
Via Torino.
🏨 1 ⬆

CORSO MAGENTA TO SANT'AMBROGIO

■ Ariosto
€€€
VIA ARIOSTO 22
TEL 02 4817844
hotelariosto.com
Ideally located for visiting Santa
Maria delle Grazie and for
shopping on Corso Vercelli.
🏨 48 ⬆ 📶 📶 *All major cards*

■ **Hotel Pierre Milano**
€€€
VIA EDMONDO DE AMICIS 32
TEL 02 72000581
hotelpierremilano.it
Excellent location, between
Sant'Ambrogio and Ticinese, and
a good quality/price ratio.
🛈 *47* 🔄 ❄ 📺 🏊 🚗 *All major cards*

■ **Antica Locanda Leonardo**
€€
CORSO MAGENTA 78
TEL 02 48014197
anticalocandaleonardo.com
A three-star hotel, welcoming
and peaceful, overlooking a
beautiful courtyard garden. The
rooms are all different and the
furnishings traditional.
🛈 *14* 🔄 🚗 *All major cards*

■ **Ostello Bello**
€
VIA MEDICI 3
TEL 02 36582720
ostellobello.com
A well-kept and friendly hostel
in a very central location. The
accommodation, arranged in
dormitories or in private rooms, is
excellent, as is the breakfast.
🔄 ❄ 🚗 *All major cards*

AROUND PARCO SEMPIONE

■ **Antica Locanda dei Mercanti**
€€€€
VIA SAN TOMASO 6
TEL 02 8054080
locanda.it
Access to this boutique hotel is
through an 18th-century palazzo.
All is very light and airy, and
furnished with great freshness
as in the choice of fabrics: white

cotton, linen, and gauze. Four
rooms have a terrace.
🛈 *15* 🔄 ❄ 🚗 *All major cards*

■ **Camperio House**
€€€€
VIA CAMPERIO 9
TEL 02 3032 2800
camperio.com
This small hotel, set in a former
convent, has plenty of charm.
There are bedrooms with en
suite bathrooms as well as
apartments.
🛈 *22* 🔄 ❄ 🚗 *All major cards*

■ **Alle Meraviglie**
€€€
VIA SAN TOMASO 6
TEL 02 8051023
allemeraviglie.it
Six romantic rooms make up this
small hotel, situated between
the Duomo and the Castello
Sforzesco.
🛈 *6* 🔄 ❄ 🚗 *All major cards*

■ **Casa Calicantus**
€€
VIA MACHIAVELLI 8
TEL 02 4814693
casacalicantus.it
This family house with coffered
ceilings has been converted to
take in guests. Enjoy the garden.
🛈 *4* 🚗 *All major cards*

TICINESE & NAVIGLI

■ **The Yard Milan**
€€€€
PIAZZA XXIV MAGGIO 8
TEL 02 89415901
theyardmilano.com
This boutique hotel in
the Darsena district offers
"distinguished guests" elegant
themed rooms, combining design

and vintage furniture.
🛈 *14* 🅿 🔄 ❄ 🚗 *All major cards*

■ **Maison Borella**
€€€
ALZAIA NAVIGLIO GRANDE 8
TEL 02 58109114
hotelmaisonborella.com
Overlooking the Naviglio
Grande, this hotel is the perfect
synthesis of the two characters
of the district: old Milan as
represented by apartment
blocks with balconies built
around a central courtyard,
and the modern capital of
design, as reflected by the
Tortona district.
🛈 *25* 🔄 ❄ 🚗 *All major cards*

■ **nhow Milano**
€€€
VIA TORTONA 35
TEL 02 4898861
nhow-milan.com
This hotel, a design icon in
Milan, also acts as a gallery
with exhibition facilities in the
communal areas. It recently
opened a popular lounge-bar,
designed by interior architect
Karim Rashid.
🛈 *246* 🔄 ❄ 🚗 *All major cards*

■ **Gogolostello**
€
VIA CHIETI 1
TEL 02 36755522
gogolostello.it
Low-cost but welcoming, this
modest hostel also offers a
literary café.
🛈 *7* 🔄 ❄ 🚗 *All major cards*

INDEX

INDEX

INDEX

CREDITS

Cover (UP), Catarina Belova/
Shutterstock; **Cover (LO)**, Supertrooper/
Shutterstock; **Spine**, Prawit Siriwong/
Shutterstock; **Back Cover**, iStock.com/
Aleksander Mirski; **2-3**, Simone Simone/
Shutterstock; **4**, Marcello Bertinetti; **5
(UP)**, Veneranda Biblioteca Ambrosiana/
De Agostini Picture Library; **5 (CT)**,
Marcello Bertinetti; **5 (LO)**, Saporetti/
De Agostini Picture Library; **6**, By
kind permission Museo Poldi Pezzoli;
9, Stefano Tinti/Shutterstock.com;
12-13, By kind permission Scandurra
Studio Architettura; **14**, Angelo Cavalli/
Getty Images; **15 (LE)**, G. Nimatallah/
De Agostini Picture Library; **15 (RT)**,
Giulio Veggi/Archivio White Star; **16**,
By kind permission Veneranda Fabbrica
del Duomo di Milano; **18**, Veneranda
Biblioteca Ambrosiana/G. Cigolini/
De Agostini Picture Library; **19 (UP)**,
By kind permission Veneranda Fabbrica
del Duomo di Milano; **19 (LO)**, By kind
permission Museo del Novecento/
Comune di Milano; **20 (LE & RT)**, G.
Cigolini/De Agostini Picture Library;
21, By kind permission Museo Poldi
Pezzoli; **24**, By kind permission Alcatraz
Milano; **25 (UP)**, By kind permission
Agostino Osio/HangarBicocca, Milano;
25 (LO), Boris-B/Shutterstock.com; **28**,
Nicholas Burns/The Crowded Planet;
29 (UP), Fondazione Muba; **29 (LO)**, C.
Baraggi/De Agostini Picture Library; **30**,
By kind permission Moira Ricci/Museo
Nazionale della Scienza e della Tecnologia
Leonardo Da Vinci; **32 (UP)**, Lorenzo De
Simone/Tips Images; **32 (LO)**, Hermes
Images/Tips Images; **33**, pcruciatti/
Shutterstock.com; **34**, Atlantide
Phototravel/Corbis; **36-37**, Sergey
Dzyuba/Shutterstock; **40**, Marcello
Bertinetti; **42**, Luciano Mortula/123rf;
43 (UP), By kind permission Museo
del Novecento, Comune di Milano; **43
(LO)**, By kind permission Veneranda
Fabbrica del Duomo di Milano; **44**,
C. Sappa/De Agostini Picture Library;
47, iStock.com/acprints; **48**, By kind
permission Veneranda Fabbrica del
Duomo di Milano; **50**, iStock.com/
yula; **51**, Catwalking/Getty Images; **53**,
Federico Rostagno/Shutterstock.com;
54, Marcello Bertinetti; **56**, C. Baraggi/
De Agostini Picture Library; **57 (UP)**, By

kind permission © BRESCIA/AMISANO/
Teatro alla Scala, Milano; **57 (LO)**, By
kind permission Gallerie d'Italia Intesa
San Paolo; **58**, By kind permission Museo
Poldi Pezzoli; **61**, By kind permission
Gallerie d'Italia Intesa San Paolo; **62**, By
kind permission © BRESCIA/AMISANO/
Teatro alla Scala, Milano; **64**, G. Cigolini/
De Agostini Picture Library; **65** G.
Cigolini/De Agostini Picture Library; **67**,
pcruciatti/Shutterstock.com; **68**, Marcello
Bertinetti; **70 (LE)**, Nicholas Burns/
The Crowded Planet; **70 (RT)**, AGF Srl/
Alamy; **71**, By kind permission Francesco
Arena/Fondazione Serbelloni; **72**, By
kind permission GAM Galleria d'Arte
Moderna, Comune di Milano; **74**, By kind
permission Palazzo Isimbardi, Provincia di
Milano; **76**, Eddy Buttarelli/Cuboimages;
78, Giulio Veggi/Archivio White Star;
79, De Agostini Picture Library; **81**,
By kind permission Bar Basso, Milano;
82, Marcello Bertinetti; **84**, By kind
permission Comunità Ebraica di Milano;
85 (UP), By kind permission Fondazione
MUBA; **85 (LO)**, By kind permission
Università degli studi di Milano; **86**, By
kind permission Fondazione MUBA;
88, Marcello Bertinetti; **90**, By kind
permission Università degli studi di
Milano; **92**, W. Buss/De Agostini
Picture Library; **93**, michelangeloop/
Shutterstock.com; **95**, By kind permission
QC Terme, Milano; **96**, G. Cigolini/
De Agostini Picture Library; **98**, Stefania
D'Alessandro/Getty Images; **99 (LE)**,
G. Nimatallah/De Agostini Picture
Library; **99 (RT)**, Roland Nagy/123rf;
100, Giuseppe Masci/Tips Images;
103, Eugenio Maronguiu/Shutterstock;
105, Gimas/Shutterstock.com; **106**, G.
Cigolini/De Agostini Picture Library; **108**,
Vincenzo Lombardo/Getty Images; **109**,
Nora Roitberg/Auditorium di Milano;
111, By kind permission 10 Corso Como,
Milano; **112**, Marcello Bertinetti; **114
(UP)**, G. Cigolini/Veneranda Biblioteca
Ambrosiana/De Agostini Picture Library;
114 (LO), W. Buss/De Agostini Picture
Library; **115**, G. Cigolini/De Agostini
Picture Library; **116**, Marcello Bertinetti;
119, By kind permission Fondazione
Emilio Carlo Mangini/Museo Mangini
Bonomi; **120**, C. Baraggi/De Agostini
Picture Library; **122**, De Agostini Picture

Library; **124**, andersphoto/Shutterstock;
125, Prisma/Press/De Agostini Picture
Library; **127**, By kind permission Agostino
Osio/HangarBicocca, Milano; **128**,
Marcello Bertinetti; **130**, G. Cigolini/
De Agostini Picture Library; **131 (UP)**,
Saporetti/De Agostini Picture Library;
131 (LO), By kind permission Mauro
Fermariello/Museo Nazionale della
Scienza e della Tecnologia Leonardo Da
Vinci; **132**, Saporetti/De Agostini Picture
Library; **134**, David Pearson/Alamy;
135, Vittorio Valletta/Tips Images; **136**,
By kind permission Mauro Fermariello/
Museo Nazionale della Scienza e della
Tecnologia Leonardo Da Vinci; **138**,
Massimo Borchi/Atlantide Phototravel/
Corbis; **140**, iStock.com/Buba1955; **141**,
HALTADEFINIZIONE IMAGE BANK
by kind permission Soprintendenza per
i Beni Architettonici e Paesaggistici di
Milano; **143**, Rikard Stadler/Shutterstock;
144, Angelo Cavalli/Marka; **146 (LE)**,
C. Baraggi/De Agostini Picture Library;
146 (RT), C. Sappa/De Agostini
Picture Library; **147**, By kind permission
Nicoletta Ancona/Archivio fotografico
dell'Acquario di Milano; **149**, By kind
permission Mauro Mariani/Archivio
fotografico dell'Acquario di Milano; **151**,
Ugo Ratti/Tips Images;
154, G. Cigolini/De Agostini Picture
Library; **156**, De Agostini Picture
Library; **157**, Metis e Mida Informatica/
Veneranda Biblioteca Ambrosiana/
De Agostini Picture Library; **159**, By
kind permission ADSI Cortili aperti
Palazzo Morando Attendolo Bolognini;
160, Marcello Bertinetti; **162 (LE)**, R.
Carnovalini/De Agostini Picture Library;
162 (RT), By kind permission Francesco
Maria Colombo/Fondazione Arnaldo
Pomodoro; **163**, A. De Gregorio/
De Agostini Picture Library; **165**, C.
Baraggi/De Agostini Picture Library;
167, Alexandra Lande/Shutterstock;
168, By kind permission Francesco
Carlo Tettamanzi/Fondazione Arnaldo
Pomodoro; **170**, C. Sappa/De Agostini
Picture Library; **172**, By kind permission
Salone Internazionale del Mobile di
Milano; **173**, By kind permission Salone
Internazionale del Mobile di Milano;
175, Antonio Attini/Archivio White Star;
176-177 Michal Bednarek/123

Walking Milan
Fabrizia Villa

Published by the National Geographic Society
Gary E. Knell, *President and Chief Executive Officer*
John M. Fahey, *Chairman of the Board*
Declan Moore, *Chief Media Officer*
Chris Johns, *Chief Content Officer*

Prepared by the Book Division
Hector Sierra, *Senior Vice President and General Manager*
Lisa Thomas, *Senior Vice President and Editorial Director*
Jonathan Halling, *Creative Director*
Marianne R. Koszorus, *Design Director*
Barbara A. Noe, *Senior Editor*
R. Gary Colbert, *Production Director*
Jennifer A. Thornton, *Director of Managing Editorial*
Susan S. Blair, *Director of Photography*
Meredith C. Wilcox, *Director, Administration and Rights Clearance*

Staff for This Book
Mary Norris, *Project Editor*
Elisa Gibson, *Art Director*
Moira Haney, *Senior Photo Editor*
Tim Jepson, *Contributing Writer*
Marty Ittner, *Contributing Designer*
Margherita Ragg, *Contributing Researcher*
Nicolas P. Rosenbach, *Cartographer Consultant*
Marshall Kiker, *Associate Managing Editor*
Mike O'Connor, *Production Editor*
Mike Horenstein, *Production Manager*
Katie Olsen, *Design Production Specialist*
Nicole Miller, *Design Production Assistant*
Bobby Barr, *Manager, Production Services*

Staff for De Agostini Libri S.p.A.
Laura Accomazzo, Giorgio Ferrero, *Editorial Staff*
Paola Piacco, *Graphic Design*
Geo4Map s.r.l. – Novara, *Map Production*
Rosetta Translations SARL, *Translation*

The information in this book has been carefully checked and to the best of our knowledge is accurate. However, details are subject to change, and the National Geographic Society cannot be responsible for such changes, or for errors or omissions. Assessments of sites, hotels, and restaurants are based on the author's subjective opinions, which do not necessarily reflect the publisher's opinion.

The National Geographic Society is one of the world's largest nonprofit scientific and educational organizations. Founded in 1888 to "increase and diffuse geographic knowledge," the member-supported Society works to inspire people to care about the planet. Through its online community, members can get closer to explorers and photographers, connect with other members around the world, and help make a difference. National Geographic reflects the world through its magazines, television programs, films, music and radio, books, DVDs, maps, exhibitions, live events, school publishing programs, interactive media, and merchandise. *National Geographic* magazine, the Society's official journal, published in English and 38 local-language editions, is read by more than 60 million people each month. The National Geographic Channel reaches 440 million households in 171 countries in 38 languages. National Geographic Digital Media receives more than 25 million visitors a month. National Geographic has funded more than 10,000 scientific research, conservation, and exploration projects and supports an education program promoting geography literacy. For more information, visit www.nationalgeographic.com.

For more information, please call 1-800-NGS LINE (647-5463) or write to the following address:

National Geographic Society
1145 17th Street NW
Washington, D.C. 20036-4688 U.S.A.

Your purchase supports our nonprofit work and makes you part of our global community. Thank you for sharing our belief in the power of science, exploration, and storytelling to change the world. To activate your member benefits, complete your free membership profile at natgeo.com/joinnow.

For information about special discounts for bulk purchases, please contact National Geographic Books Special Sales: ngspecsales@ngs.org

For rights or permissions inquiries, please contact National Geographic Books Subsidiary Rights: ngbookrights@ngs.org

WS White Star Publishers® is a registered trademark property of De Agostini Libri S.p.A.

ISBN: 978-1-4262-1640-4
Printed in Hong Kong
15/THK/1